Labor Shortage *Solutions*

The Business Leader's Guide to Maximizing Employee Potential

Bill Conerly

Labor Shortage Solutions:
The Business Leader's Guide to Maximizing Employee Potential

Table of Contents

Part 1

Introduction

In 2005 I was asked to brief a group of business executives on the 10-year economic outlook. I had begun my corporate career making 20-year economic forecasts, but this work needed to add insights for business, including technology and social change.

In preparing the presentation, I looked at the demographics that would apply in the decade of the 2010s. I was stunned by how the growth of the working age population would slow down. I told the business leaders to expect a very tight labor market.

At the reception following my remarks, I asked people what they thought about the future of the labor market. Nobody was as worried as I was. When I probed a little deeper, I heard several say that they would be retired by the time it became a problem.

After that presentation, article about labor force management caught my eye. I noticed academic studies about worker productivity, consultants' reports on employee retention, and popular business press columns about recruiting techniques. I began connecting dots between the economic statistics I review daily and the business practices that work best for employee productivity, retention and recruiting.

As the years passed, we saw rising unemployment in the Great Recession, followed by a slow rebound. Gradually, unemployment fell. As I continued to speak with business leaders, I heard more and more comments about the difficulty they were having hiring and retaining workers.

To illustrate the problem in 2018, I took these photographs, all within a quarter-mile stretch near my office in Oregon.

Hiring became much harder after the Covid pandemic began, then improved just a little bit. But the labor market will continue to be tight for years to come, as explained in one of my articles.

These article all appeared on Forbes.com. I have reviewed them all, and they stand the test of time, though some make references to past events that are no longer top-of-mind. I have made minor edits to correct typos and for clarity. All articles in their original form can be found at Forbes.com.

Part 2

The Labor Market Challenge

Chapter 1

The Scariest Chart For Business In The Coming Decade: Workers Not Available

Published on Forbes.com March 25, 2018

The scariest chart I've ever developed shows that the pool of available workers will grow at the slowest pace since the Civil War. If your business plans include expansion, either figure out a way to do it without more workers, or get better than other companies at employee retention and recruiting.

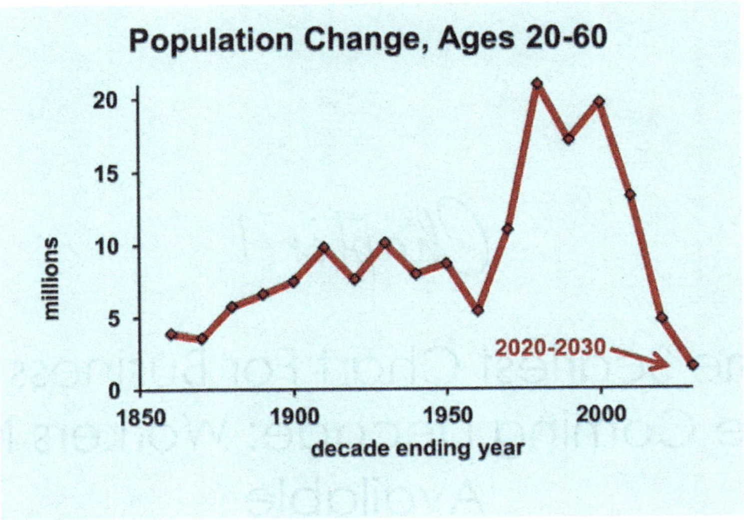

The accompanying chart shows Census Bureau figures for the working-age population every ten years from 1850. The growth in the years 2020 through 2030 will be the lowest since the Civil War. Not on a percentage basis, even, but the lowest in terms of the raw increase in the number of people aged 20 through 60. The lowest since the Civil War.

The figures in the chart got worse last week as the Census Bureau revised downward their population projections to incorporate lower foreign immigration. Actual estimates of immigration had been coming in below the previous projections, which had been issued in 2014. The updated population projections show 21 percent less immigration through 2030 than previously projected. So we knew it was going to be bad, and now it's going to be even worse.

The biggest factor behind slow growth of the working-age population is the aging of baby boomers. Keep in mind that the baby boom continued for many years, peaking in 1957 and continuing until about 1964. (The line of demarcation is fuzzy.) Afterwards, the number of births slowed down, finally rising again when the boomers had their own children.

Boomers are retiring and will continue to retire for another ten years. The millennials are mostly of working age already, and their generation was followed by a smaller number of births. So we have lots of people aging out of the workforce, and very few growing into the workforce. This is happening at a time when foreign immigration is really low.

Unemployment is currently 4.1 percent, but it's not a temporary low. The tight labor market will be a persistent challenge to business in the coming decade. Companies that thrive will either find a way to grow without expanding their workforce, or they will get really good at employee retention and recruiting. I recommend both strategies, but keep in mind that not every company can be better than average. The bar will rise as more and more businesses compete for available workers.

Improving employee retention and recruiting will be harder because today's corporate leaders have become used to an era of easy labor availability. Some companies use on-call scheduling which provides employees with little advance notice of their work hours. Restaurants may have some employees closing one night and then opening the next morning, providing little rest time in between. Businesses may tolerate first-level supervisors who show little respect for staff members. For over six years, from mid-2008 through late 2014, higher than average unemployment rates prevailed, enabling sloppy personnel practices. But those days are over, and management needs to adapt to the new reality of tight labor markets.

What's a company to do? I've written a series of articles and produced several videos on the subject. Check out Leadership In Today's Tight Labor Market: Reduce Employee Turnover, and 3 Steps To Hire With Lower Education Requirements: Coping With The Tight Labor Market. If you prefer video, go to the YouTube playlist "Leadership in Today's Tight Labor Market".

Resources:

Updated population projections: https://www.census.gov/data/tables/2017/demo/popproj/2017-summary-tables.html

Leadership In Today's Tight Labor Market: Reduce Employee Turnover: included in this volume and at http://www.forbes.com/sites/billconerly/2018/01/19/leadership-in-a-tight-labor-market-reduce-employee-turnover/

3 Steps To Hire With Lower Education Requirements: Coping With The Tight Labor Market: included in this volume and at http://www.forbes.com/sites/billconerly/2018/02/25/three-steps-to-hire-with-lower-education-requirements-coping-with-the-tight-labor-market/

Video, Leadership in Today's Tight Labor Market: https://www.youtube.com/watch?v=NIA53tDLX8g&list=PLQhBJ0F4v3hyX37Da2HnOjH3VvrW_3b32

Chapter 2

Tight Labor Market: Even Worse Based On New Census Projections

Published on Forbes.com February 22, 2020

The working age population will grow at the slowest pace since the Civil War in the decade of 2020-2030, I wrote two years ago in The Scariest Chart For Business In The Coming Decade: Workers Not Available. The outlook is even worse now, because foreign immigration is much lower than projected, meaning that even fewer working age people will be in the United States.

Last year's estimate of net immigration into the United States, counting both legal and undocumented people, was 40% lower than the Census Bureau's projections. (Their latest projections began in 2017.) Now the bureau has created alternative scenarios, including one that very closely matches recent data. It now appears based on that low-immigration alternative scenario that we'll have virtually zero growth of the working age population through 2030. (The alternative projections do not have the same detail as the base projections that I used to create the chart, but back-of-the-envelope calculations imply approximately no growth at all.)

Long-term projections can be worthwhile even if they get the first few years wrong. I began my career making 25-year forecasts, so I know the issue intimately. We can shrug off early errors due to temporary fluctuations, such as a recession. This immigration forecast error differs, in that the older Census projections assumed that recent years had been a fluke, and immigration would return to "normal." We now know that the years just prior to the projection period were the beginning of a trend to lower immigration.

The business implication is that employers will have to work even harder to retain employees and recruit new workers. The strength of the current economy aggravates the challenge, but even a slower-growing economy would leave us with insufficient people for all of the expansion plans that private companies, non-profit organizations and government agencies now have.

The recent report, "US Labor Shortages: Challenges and Solutions," by Gad Levanon's team at the Conference Board, highlights our current problems.

As a country, the U.S. could expand legal immigration to bring more people in. That's unlikely to happen anytime soon (though I don't claim to be very good at political forecasts.)

For an individual company, the solution is better labor management. That begins, as I wrote earlier, with the best employee benefit a worker can have: a good boss. (For details, take a look at my Forbes articles on leadership in a tight labor market. [The articles in this book.]

Business leaders should elevate employee retention and recruiting to the highest priority, at least if they want their companies to survive the next decade. Much of the vital work will be performed by first-level supervisors, but senior executives are vital to ensure the training, support and accountability systems needed to help the front-line managers.

In 10 years we will look back at the decade of the 2020s and see that the most successful companies excelled in labor management. And I believe that most of those successful companies will have started in 2020, if not earlier.

Resources:

The Scariest Chart For Business In The Coming Decade: Workers Not Available: https://www.forbes.com/sites/billconerly/2018/03/25/the-scariest-chart-for-business-in-the-coming-decade-workers-not-available/#7aa514513de9

Census Bureau's projections: https://www.census.gov/data/tables/2017/demo/popproj/2017-summary-tables.html

US Labor Shortages: Challenges and Solutions: https://www.conference-board.org/topics/labor-shortages

Leadership in a tight labor market: https://www.conerlyconsulting.com/2019/12/13/leadership-in-todays-tight-labor-market/

Chapter 3

More Retirements, Less Immigration Will Clobber Businesses Needing Employees

Published on Forbes.com September 29, 2020

The American labor market was very tight back in the good old days of 2019. Despite the surge in unemployment with the pandemic, some companies today have trouble hiring. Retirements have risen and foreign immigration has declined, making labor shortages even worse.

In the competition for workers, companies that lay the groundwork early will retain more good staff member and be able to recruit the additional workers they need, at the expense of businesses that waited until the last minute to address the challenge.

The central problem for the decade of the 2020s is that baby boomers retire, and the replacement generation is no larger than the departing generation. The problem was documented in The Scariest Chart For Business In The Coming Decade. Since then, Census Bureau projections worsened due to declining foreign immigration into the

United States. And those projections were made prior to the Covid-19 pandemic.

Most of the demographic change is routine: baby boomers getting older, as younger workers also grow into their working years. Two issues can change quickly, and they have both turned to worsen the labor shortage.

Foreign immigration is dramatically lower than previously, and lower than the Census Bureau projections. The Trump Administration has cut back sharply on new immigrant visas. From February through July 2020 (the most recent month for which data are available), immigrant visa issuance was 69% lower than in the same months of 2019. That means 158,000 fewer new residents. The data come from the State Department and do not include tourist visas.

The second issue is retirements. Many people have flexibility in their retirements. One factory manager reported that several older workers retired as their children advised them not to take the risk of coming into the shop. For many people, the pandemic is a time to re-evaluate life and what to do with it. And people in their sixties will often retire when they lose their jobs. Retirements can be gauged by the number of new Social Security retirement beneficiaries. February-through-July retirements ran 5.4% higher than in the same months of 2019. This decade is certainly a time when more people are turning 65 and 66, but the previous year's gain was only 3.7%. This difference is 85,000 actual workers.

With lower immigration, both now and in the next few years, the working-age population will level off. With increased retirements now, the actual number of available workers will be even lower than last year's projections.

Even today with the high unemployment rate, many companies are challenged in finding workers. Recent news reports have cited moving companies, restaurants, biotech, landscaping and manufacturing.

Companies looking to the future can ease their workforce problems by taking early action. Step one is to recognize the severity of the challenge, making employee retention and recruitment a top executive priority. The first-level managers play the most important role, but senior leadership must set expectations and evaluate performance.

Employee retention is far more important than recruiting efforts. Although the human resources field is rife with discussion of employee pay, health care and the like, the very best benefit that an employee can have is a good boss. Nothing improves retention as much. Training and accountability of first-level supervisors makes the greatest difference in employee retention..

Business leaders can read all of my Forbes articles on how to cope with the employee shortage.

Resources:

The Scariest Chart For Business In The Coming Decade: https://www.forbes.com/sites/billconerly/2018/03/25/the-scariest-chart-for-business-in-the-coming-decade-workers-not-available/

Census Bureau projections worsened: https://www.forbes.com/sites/billconerly/2020/02/22/tight-labor-market-even-worse-based-on-new-census-projections/#62eec56613f1

Data come from the State Department: https://travel.state.gov/content/travel/en/legal/visa-law0/visa-statistics/annual-reports/report-of-the-visa-office-2019.html

New Social Security retirement beneficiaries: https://www.ssa.gov/cgi-bin/awards.cgi

How to cope with the employee shortage: https://www.conerlyconsulting.com/2019/12/13/leadership-in-todays-tight-labor-market/

Chapter 4

Lowest Population Growth In Over A Century Means Tighter Labor Market For Business

Published on Forbes.com December 23, 2020

Population in the United States grew at the slowest pace since 1918, the Census Bureau reported this week. This annual estimate will be superseded by the decennial census soon, but it provides a year-over-year look that the 10-year snapshot will miss. For business leaders, as well as executives of non-profits and government agencies, the report emphasizes the fundamental labor shortage currently masked by the pandemic recession. This slow growth of the population will continue for years, with especially dire results for the labor force.

The annual population figures estimate the resident population as of July 1. The lowest growth rate prior to this year was back in 1918, when we sent two million young men to Europe in World War I. (Overseas soldiers are not counted in the resident population.) The Spanish flu also took a toll, but most deaths occurred after July 1, 1918.

Our numbers are increasing so slowly because of light natural increase and small foreign immigration. Births have been declining since 2015 as the millennials started aging out of their prime child-bearing years. Deaths have been rising as the baby boomers grow older. Even greater than these changes have been the decline in net international migration, which has dropped every year since 2016. Like it or not, President Trump's immigration policies had a substantial impact.

The latest numbers will be revised as we get results from the decennial census, and the estimates are softer than usual this year. Although we have a very good handle on the number of births and deaths, immigration is much more challenging. The Census Bureau tries to include undocumented aliens in these estimates. The bureau gets hard data on visas issued to immigrants but has to use much weaker information for the undocumented migrants. We also lack good data on the outflow of people from the United States to other countries. Some of the movement consists of U.S. citizens becoming ex-pats abroad, but an even great number are foreign-born residents returning to their homelands. Despite the soft data, the latest figures accord with prior years' trend and what we know about the country's population drivers in the latest year.

Business sales won't increase as much with slower population growth, so companies should adjust their expectations downward a small amount. Companies serving the markets related to life and death should adjust their own market estimates, downward for births and upwards for funerals.

The greatest business impact of the demographic changes will be tighter labor markets. The unemployment rate rose when the pandemic triggered layoffs, but changed little for jobs that can be performed remotely. With the vaccine soon to help many sectors of the economy, the labor market will tighten up again.

The new relief bill will send an extra $300 a week to those collecting unemployment insurance, meaning that those who had been making less than $15 an hour, approximately, will be better off not working than back on the job. The threshold is even lower for previously part-time workers. (The specifics vary from state to state.)

The upshot of the latest news is that employee retention and recruitment will be even more important in 2021 than it has been in past years.

Resources:

Census Bureau reported: https://www.census.gov/newsroom/press-releases/2020/estimates-population-housing-units.html

Chapter 5

Demographics And Remote Work: Intertwined Challenges For Business

Published on Forbes.com June 5, 2021

Workers and managers will face twin challenges in the coming years: adjusting to what we've learned about remote work, and the demographic change to low growth of the working age population. Each will be a challenge, and the interaction of the two will require managers to test their assumptions, adapt, and re-test.

Demographics is the less recognized issue for the workplace in the 2020s. Baby boomers will retire in greater numbers in the coming years. The boom in births lasted from 1946 through 1962, so the later boomers will hit age 65 in 2027. The group turning 25 years old this decade is about the same size as the preceding cohort. So we in the U.S. will see no increase in young people entering their working years and more boomers retiring. Other countries will have similar experience, though magnitudes and timing vary around the world.

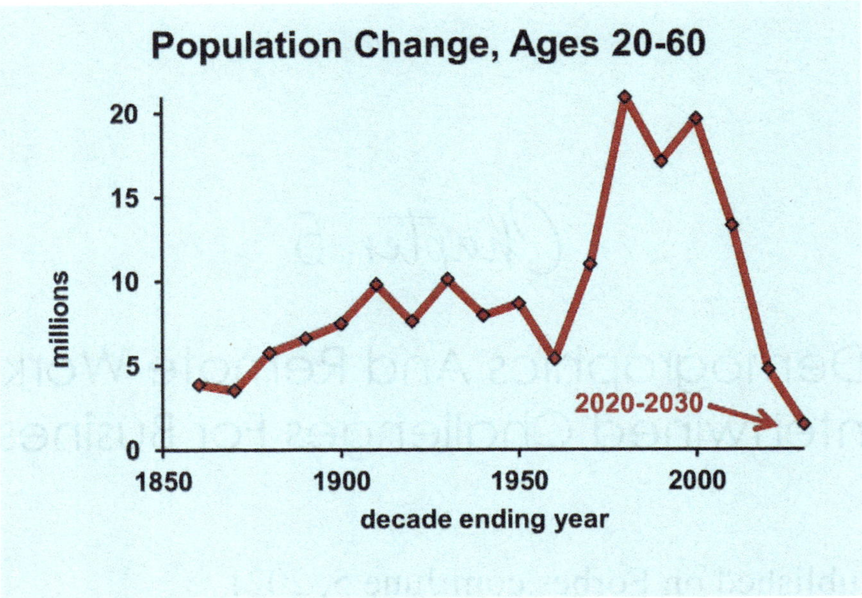

The only hope for growth of the working-age population is immigration—which in the U.S. has plunged in recent years. As a percent of the existing population, net international migration was 0.15% for the year ending July 1, 2020, half as much as five years prior. And most of the last data year was pre-pandemic. When we get the next data point, it will certainly be lower.

President Biden's administration has not changed immigration policy from the Trump era, though the president is far more polite than his predecessor. Nobody in Washington seems to want a significant increase in foreign immigration. That means the working age population won't grow over this decade. (Growth will resume in the 2030s.)

Businesses hoping to expand in size—and employment—will find that employee recruiting and retention are their greatest challenges.

Into that environment is our discovery during the pandemic that people can work from home successfully. A Stanford economist estimated that

51% of all jobs could be done remotely. Some workers liked working from home while others were eager to return to offices, with another significant portion wanting both: some days working from home and some days in the office.

Managers are spread out on the question of the ideal balance of office and remote work, according to a PWC survey. Employees, too, vary widely in their preferences according to the same study.

Most analysts expect a hybrid model, in which the office is available to everyone every day, and mandatory some number of days a week. Managers seem more eager to have their workers back in the office, while many workers are much less eager.

The varying preferences for remote work by managers will collide with the demographically-driven tight labor market. Managerial preferences cannot dominate unless they are related to productivity, though some managers probably don't realize that now.

If remote work is less productive than office work, then managers will need to balance ease of recruitment of remote workers against higher productivity of office workers.

But if remote work is just as productive, then managers will have to cater to employees who prefer to work remotely. Otherwise they'll have to pay up in salary, as well as office expenses, with no productivity gain to offset the cost.

Managers will then be challenged to figure out just how much more productive office workers are, if at all. Right now many business executives are working from anecdotes and preconceptions, pretty much guessing about productivity. The best managers will use hard data when available, and good judgment the rest of the time.

In the executive suite, top leaders of the organization need to understand the challenges that line managers face. One-size-fits-all company policies about remote work will limit managers' ability to fit the rules to the work. Companies that force the work to fit the rules will have lower productivity and higher costs. They will fail in the hyper-competitive market for workers.

Either of these two challenges, demographics and remote work, would tax even the best managers. Having them intertwine requires that employee retention and recruitment become top priority for leaders of all companies.

Resources:

Stanford economist estimated: https://news.stanford.edu/2020/06/29/snapshot-new-working-home-economy/

PWC survey: https://www.pwc.com/us/en/library/covid-19/us-remote-work-survey.html shows no consensus on the back-to-work model

Chapter 6

Drop In U.S. Immigration Further Tightens Labor Market

Published on Forbes.com April 28, 2022

Foreign immigration into the United States is unusually low, a fact easily missed by news photos of people trying to cross the Rio Grande River. Government policy cut the number of immigrant visas granted, then the Covid-19 restrictions further reduced the number of foreigners coming into the country. The decline in immigration will keep the labor market tight for some years to come.

The Census Bureau reported that three major factors were at work in last year's immigration: declining immigration of foreign-born people, increasing exits of foreign-born from the U.S., and changes in Puerto Rican movement after Hurricane Maria in 2017. Part of the drop in immigration resulted from Trump-era rules, while Covid-19 also played a significant rule. But the downward trend started in 2017, and by 2019 net foreign immigration into the United States had dropped almost in half.

The data are imperfect. Net foreign immigration—adding incoming residents and subtracting outgoing—includes estimates of undocumented immigration. The annual data don't always align with the decennial census, so some massaging of the numbers occurs. But even with some inaccuracy, the change in immigration is stark.

The decline in immigration comes while baby boomers are aging out of their working years. Last year the working age population (ages 25-65) actually declined, though by a tiny percentage. The drop in working age population came while demand for goods and services grew rapidly, as the country's consumers, businesses and governments were flush with cash. The labor shortage is no surprise.

The outlook for the labor market is grim for employers but very bright for job seekers. The demographics of baby boomers retiring means that in this decade, there will be no net gain in the working age population absent substantial immigration.

The prospects for increased legal immigration are low. Donald Trump connected with working class people antagonistic toward immigration. Republicans in the past reflected business preference for a larger workforce, until Trump won the White House. Now Republicans are mostly focusing on the anti-immigration voters rather than pro-immigration businesses. Democrats have generally been less favorable toward immigration because of their close ties to labor unions that don't want competition from low-wage immigrants. Few pro-immigration voices are heard these days. So it's unlikely that immigration will rise much in the years ahead.

Official Census Bureau projections show this decade, from 2020 through 2030, will have the lowest growth of the working age population since the Civil War. And those projections were made in 2017, before we had the data to show that 2016 was the immigration peak. The projections looked for net foreign immigration of around one million people per year. We had less than a quarter million last year. In other words, the projections that show extremely low growth in the working age population are overly optimistic.

The business implication is straightforward. Success in this entire decade will depend on great achievements in employee retention, employee recruiting and employee productivity. Average performing companies will struggle, while below-average companies will fail. This labor challenge will overwhelm other business challenges for years to come.

Chapter 7

New Census Projections Show Tight Labor Market For Years

Published on Forbes.com November 9, 2023

The U.S. Census Bureau issued new long-term population projections which are gloomy for employers. The growth of the working age population in the current decade, from 2020 to 2030, will be the lowest since the Civil War. These projections indicate even less labor force growth than the previous figures, which were released in 2018. Lower immigration than previously expected dominates the labor force issue. The Census Bureau believes immigration in future years will be about 17% lower than they previously projected—which itself was lower than 2014 projections.

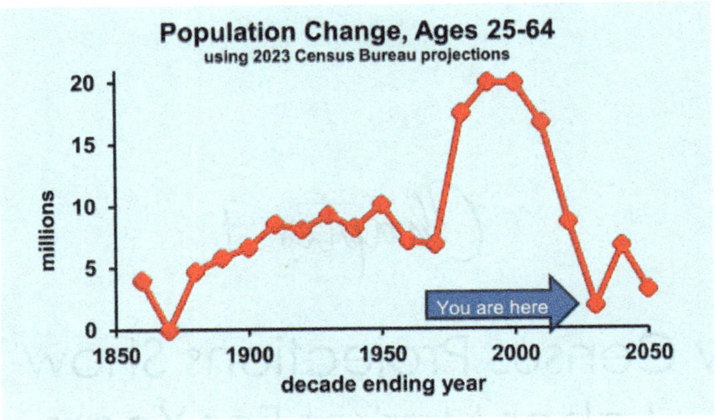

Hiring and retaining workers will be a dog-eat-dog, employer-eat-employer effort. The ability to succeed in this competition will differentiate successful companies from laggards. The keys to business success in this environment are employee productivity, retention and recruiting—in that order.

Attitudes About Employment

Before specific strategy steps are considered, business leaders should examine how their own attitudes align with the challenge. In the chart above, notice the four decades of high growth in the working-age population. Those are years from 1970 through 2010. The baby boomers were coming of age, and then their children came of age. The chart does not show the other huge change: women in the workforce. In 1970, there were 32 million women in the workforce (either working or actively looking for work). By 2010, the number was 72 million.

That abundance of people available to work led managers to treat workers as disposable. If one didn't work out, there were plenty of other applicants available. That's obviously an overstatement, but it's certainly true that development of skills and retention of talent took a lower priority because of the many people looking for work. Business leaders now must develop an attitude that labor is scarce and to be nurtured and treasured—not for charitable reasons, but to get the job done.

Worker Productivity

Productivity of workers is the most important element in business strategy for the tight labor market. Productivity does not usually mean exhortations or threats or pep talks. Rather, training, tools and management should dominate productivity efforts.

Training usually begins at the beginning, but continued training will help experienced workers be even more productive. People cannot absorb everything all at once, so staggered and continuous training helps employees achieve their potential.

Tools are vital in virtually every job, whether the tools are screwdrivers, software or trucks. A focus on how the tool helps productivity ensures that capital spending is not just for shiny toys, and not for excessive complexity, but getting more work accomplished by a given worker.

Good management helps productivity by putting the right person on the right job at the right time. Good managers know their workers well, including their strengths and weaknesses. They can coach weak workers, but more importantly they can nurture moderately good workers and motivate excellent workers to do even more.

Employee Retention

Retaining good and even average employees boosts overall output and lowers costs. The old saw that "people don't quit companies, they quit bosses," is true. Better training of first-level supervisors helps employee retention more than fancy fringe benefits. Stay Interviews—once managers are trained in the process—help retention.

Compensation, both salary and fringe benefits, must be competitive, but need not be higher than market. Too many managers accept a departing employee's explanation that he found 50 cents an hour more at another company. The manager must ask herself, why did this worker go looking for a 50 cent pay raise? Most likely, better managerial skills could have kept the worker.

Retention is much easier when the right people are hired in the first place. Sometimes managers get desperate, especially when a valuable employee has just left. Desperate hires, though, seldom work out. Each job requires specific skills from the employee, but more importantly certain attitudes and personalities. Finding the person who will embrace the company culture and values usually works much better than the wrong personality who seems to have the right skills.

Employee Recruiting

Even with good productivity and retention, new hires will be needed. Hiring is easier when employee retention is good. Satisfied employees are more likely to recommend their companies to friends and acquaintances. So the retention steps outlined above are the first steps to better recruiting.

In decades past, many businesses simply waited until someone walked in the door, or they put a "Help Wanted" sign outside their shop, or advertised in the newspaper. In today's tight labor market, recruiting requires a marketing strategy. How can a company attract the people who will find working at the company satisfying? In the coming years, marketing to prospective employees will be nearly as important as marketing to prospective customers.

This new world of tight labor availability is not about the pandemic. Consider the conclusion that this decade is having the lowest growth of the population since the Civil War. That showed up in the 2018 projections, just not as prominently as in today's projections. Employers have a long slog ahead of them, which won't be much easier for many years.

Resources:

New long-term population projections: https://www.census.gov/data/tables/2023/demo/popproj/2023-summary-tables.html

Stay Interviews: https://www.forbes.com/sites/billconerly/2018/07/21/retain-more-employees-with-stay-interviews/

Part 3

Improving Labor Productivity

Chapter 8

Strategies For Increasing Employee Productivity With Better Tools

Published on Forbes.com January 9, 2024

The labor market will continue to be tight for employers over the remainder of the decade, as Census projections show. Hiring became a bit easier in 2023, but the long-run demographics will constrain employment growth for many years. For companies trying to operate, and even grow, in this environment, better employee retention will help a lot, better recruiting will help a little, but the best solution comes from better productivity.

Raising employee productivity—output per hour worked—comes not by threatening workers with firing: they know they can get another job right away in a tight labor market. Incentives to boost production may work for a little while, but many employee responsibilities cannot be measured well enough for production bonuses. Instead, the path to better productivity involves better tools, better training and better management.

This article focuses on better tools, using the word broadly to include software and computer systems as well as wrenches and pencils. Although wage rates have risen, the cost of some tools used by employees has fallen or leveled off. Thus, the value of boosting productivity has grown faster than the cost in many cases.

The companies most successful at increasing employee productivity use two different approaches, in tandem, to identify the tools that will help their workers. The first is talking to employees. The manager asks, "What are the slow, tedious tasks that might be sped up?" The second approach uses a broader perspective than the worker might have about what possible tools exist.

Conversations between supervisors and employees should be regular events, but often aren't, or they only deal with problems. At least annually, the boss should ask what could make the employee's work easier or faster or more accurate. The question should be phrased not as an employee performance question but as an inquiry about tools and the work environment.

Sometimes a worker knows that productivity would be higher with a new tool—maybe a cordless screwdriver, maybe a computer app—but the person is not comfortable asking the boss. The employee has been provided with tools and should do the job with the tools provided, the thinking goes. But the manager may have a different view: A $50 expenditure is trivial compared to the cost of the employee's time.

Workers will sometimes know that a task is slow and tedious but will not have an idea for speeding up the process. That's why the second approach is necessary: providing a broader perspective. The manager may know right away what a good solution is, even if the employee doesn't. But in other cases, the manager may need to bring in outside help. For example, if an employee is spending hours plowing through a complicated database, an IT professional might suggest a new computer application that neither the employee or direct supervisor are aware of.

What sorts of tools will improve productivity? Communications tools can help, ranging from text to voice to video messaging systems. Mobility tools include laptops, tablets and cell phone apps. Routing programs can tell a service driver with multiple stops to make which order to place the locations in.

Many office workers would benefit from better software, especially apps that perform repetitive tasks. Very few Excel users are comfortable writing macros, but most would benefit from a few good ones customized to their particular tasks. Good information systems—with easy search and reporting functions—will help many employees in their daily tasks.

For work with physical objects (such as in manufacturing and construction), think about hand tools, electric tools, pneumatic tools. Consider better ergonomics so that employees don't tire so quickly or have a position enabling greater accuracy.

With the tight labor market continuing for years, the best time to improve productivity is now, and providing better tools for employees is a great first step.

Resources:

Census projections show:
https://www.forbes.com/sites/billconerly/2023/11/09/new-census-projections-show-tight-us-labor-market-for-years/

Chapter 9

Strategies For Improving Labor Productivity Through Employee Training

Published on Forbes.com February 1, 2024

The labor market will be tight through the end of the decade, making employee recruiting and retention difficult. Boosting the output of employees is the best strategy for coping with the difficult labor environment. The three strategies for productivity improvement are better tools, better training and better management. This article focuses on how training can help employees produce more.

Training can be a drag on productivity. Most corporate employees have sat through dull, boring training sessions that did not help their work abilities but did subtract from productive time. Value comes from the right training for the right employees at the right time.

Selecting the most useful training is like upgrading tools to boost employee productivity: Workers' thoughts about their needs should be combined with expert opinion. An added twist to training is that it can help employees in their current roles as well as prepare them for future roles.

The process will vary depending on whether a particular task is performed by just one worker or by many. A business might have hundreds of customer service representatives but just one treasury manager. For the large occupation, a sample of conversations can identify training needs that employees perceive. For the lone job, an individual conversation must be held.

When beginning the conversation, the manager's tone should stress the company's desire to help the employee rather than dissatisfaction with current performance. Some employees will be able to say exactly what additional training would help them perform their job better. In many or most cases, though, the employee won't be able to describe the training needed. The supervisor should discuss the particular tasks that seem to take a lot of time, either time to do the job or time to get it done right.

This is where expertise in training resources comes into play. The manager—or another person familiar with training options—should identify the particular training that would help the employee.

For groups, it will certainly be the case that not everyone needs the same training. For a new software system, maybe everyone needs to start with the same training program. But some will catch on quickly, while others will need longer training. Individualizing training plans to specific employees' needs and abilities will upgrade productivity without wasting excessive time. Coming back to that customer service example, some employees might benefit from better product knowledge, while others would gain from improved listening practices. One-size-fits-all usually fits very poorly.

The second goal of training should be preparing employees for future positions. A winning approach is to look at front-line workers doing a good job and inviting them to managerial training. All too often employees are promoted when a vacancy occurs, and the employee has to come up to speed on new responsibilities without really understanding how to lead people. In other instances, though, just-in-time training will work.

The training strategy should also consider hard-to-fill positions. For example, if a construction company has trouble finding good welders, it might consider inviting a bright, hard-working unskilled worker to train for that position. The company might offer to cover the cost of the training if the worker does it on his or her own time. Or the company might pick up both tuition and time spent training.

Cross-functional training usually does not improve productivity in the near term, but it can help to prevent disasters. No employee is immune to disease and injury. Every manager's responsibility includes planning for sudden, unexpected absences of key employees. Additional training may be necessary before there's a problem.

Many types of training might help productivity. Some would be quite specific, like training on best use of a tool or software. Other would be more general, such as communication, teamwork or problem-solving.

Coaching is a form of training that can benefit both parties. For instance, an experienced worker could coach another employee. Coaching is usually an occasional activity rather than full time. It could be scheduled, such as an hour a week, or impromptu as needed. Coaches often benefit from the experience. They must think through how they perform a function or handle problems. Some things they have been doing instinctively may improve when the coaches are compelled to explain step-by-step.

In a tight labor market, improving worker productivity through training can boost company competitiveness. But the training must be focused on specific employee challenges rather than generalized feel-good programs.

Resources:

Labor market will be tight:
https://www.forbes.com/sites/billconerly/2023/11/09/new-census-projections-show-tight-us-labor-market-for-years/

Tools to boost employee productivity:
https://www.forbes.com/sites/billconerly/2024/01/09/strategies-for-increasing-employee-productivity-with-better-tools/

Chapter 10

Strategies for Improving Employee Productivity Through Manager Training

Published on Forbes.com on March 8, 2024

Business managers will continue to be challenged by the tight labor market for many years to come, as my previous articles have shown. The three key strategies for dealing with this problem entail increasing employee productivity, improving retention and better recruiting, in that order. Employee productivity can be increased without pushing people harder, but by providing better tools, targeted employee training, and improved training of first-level managers, which is the subject of this article.

Managers make very large contributions to employee productivity, at least when they are on top of their game. They bring new workers up to speed, correct mistakes in a way that leads to fewer mistakes in the future, bring out the best in good performers and make everyone feel appreciated for excellent work. Just as employee training can make employees more productive, the right training for first-level managers will boost their ability to help front-line employees be more productive.

As with many initiatives, asking the managers themselves about their training needs should begin the process. Conversations about the initiative should note the goal: increasing employee productivity, such as output per work-hour or achieving quality goals.

Managers' opinions can then be enhanced with outside ideas appropriate to the kind of work the employees do. One of the most valuable is performance management, which involves setting clear performance goals, providing regular feedback, coaching and encouragement. I have asked many employees in different types of jobs if they get enough feedback on their performance from their bosses. Nobody has yet reported getting too much feedback, but many have said they get very little.

Effective communication training will often help supervisors with performance management as well as more routine exchanges. In any company, some managers are probably doing a good job at communicating, while others are not. This illustrates that executives may want to tailor training to particular managers.

Leadership skills help managers motivate employees to do great work. Motivation like a high school pep rally will probably have little lasting impact, but good leaders help employees look forward to another day of on the job.

Conflict resolution works like an obscure tool in a mechanic's toolbox. When it is needed, there's nothing else that works. Problem employees sap the motivation from all of the good workers around them. Managers need to know when they have an issue and how to deal with it.

Other managerial training options are dependent on the type of work involved. For some, team-building will pay great dividends. In other cases, it will have little impact on employee productivity. Similarly, time management and delegation will be important in some circumstances but not others.

Training of managers should be on-going. Many good lessons must be repeated and reinforced. And some potentially good lessons are lost until the employee has the experience to utilize them. As the manager gains greater understanding of the role and the challenges, different training needs will arise. In this area, selection of the most impactful training must continuously evolve.

Resources:

Previous articles:
https://www.forbes.com/sites/billconerly/2023/11/09/new-census-projections-show-tight-us-labor-market-for-years/

Better tools:
https://www.forbes.com/sites/billconerly/2024/01/09/strategies-for-increasing-employee-productivity-with-better-tools/

Targeted Employee training:
https://www.forbes.com/sites/billconerly/2024/02/01/strategies-for-improving-labor-productivity-through-employee-training/

Part 4

Improving Labor Retention

Chapter 11

Quits Are Up: 7 Employee Retention Strategies Your Company Must Have

Published on Forbes.com December 11, 2013

Over two and a quarter million employees quit their jobs in October, the highest number since 2010. Are your staff members going to sing Johnny Paycheck's best song, "Take This Job and Shove It?"

With low quit rates the last few years, managers could get away with being poor managers. With the economy improving, however, we'll learn the wisdom of Warren Buffett's comment (from a different context): "You only find out who is swimming naked when the tide goes out." You'll only know which of your managers are discouraging your employees when job opportunities outside your company improve.

Here are 7 vital employee retention strategies:

1. **Track retention**. If you don't measure it, it won't improve. If you don't know which line managers are doing well and which are not, you'll not know who needs coaching. And if you don't

know where you stand relative to your industry, then you're probably one of the worst.

2. **Train first level supervisors**. I don't claim to be an HR expert, but good supervisors are crucial to retention. Steve Miranda, who is an expert, says, "Employees don't quite jobs. They quit managers." That's an overstatement, but not by much. Top on the list of best practices is regular meetings with employees about performance and expectations.

3. **Hire right in the first place**. Too many employment interviews are about personality: whether the job candidate matches the manager's personality. Focus more on job skills and you'll get a better fit, which is more likely to lead to a long employment tenure.

4. **Offer employees a path to greater pay, recognition and responsibility**. Not everyone can rise to CEO, but every employee can build skills. Find a way to recognize those skills and challenge employees to gain even more skills. That makes not only a better employee, but one who feels a sense of accomplishment and success.

5. **Look for ways to increase flexibility in work conditions**. Can you accommodate non-work responsibilities and desires of your employees? Overly rigid work rules can drive good workers away.

6. **Look for stressors**. Train leaders on how to help employees in stressful positions.

7. **Re-evaluate your benefits package**. This isn't to say that benefits need to be increased, but that the package should meet the needs of those employees most likely to leave the company.

> All too often, very senior managers think about what is important to them, not the 30-somethings who are considering changing jobs.

What's not on the list? Salary. Sometimes you need to adjust total pay, but companies usually spend too much time thinking about pay and not enough time thinking about the other issues that make employees feel good or bad about their jobs.

Chapter 12

Rule Number One For Dealing With Millennials In The Workplace

Published on Forbes.com December 17, 2017

Most of what you've heard about millennials is wrong. Well, only sort of wrong. Wrong in the same way that adult men are 5'10" tall. That is certainly the average height, but it's not me, nor is it most of my friends. Because averages are always kind of wrong, advice about millennials is kind of wrong.

Are they more interested than other generations in purpose and doing good? Sure, on average. Opportunity to learn on the job? Yes, some of them. Autonomy combined with feedback, plenty of them. But not all.

There are about 75 million people in the millennial generation. Can you imagine 75 million people with identical hopes and aspirations? Identical fears, anxieties and worries? Identical desire for human companionship versus time alone? Identical balance of greed versus concern for others?

Rule Number One for a manager working with millennials is simple: treat everyone as an individual. Learn the person's goals. Figure out how best to use the person's abilities. Coach for career development that reflects the millennial's individual uniqueness.

One size will not fit all millennials, just as it never did Baby Boomers or Gen. X. In fact, the best advice for managing millennials also works pretty well for other generations.

Broad generalizations are useful, a little. Positioning a job opening to be attractive to millennials can help recruiting. I have advised companies trying to recruit younger workers not to advertise for a "hard-charging salesman." Instead, go looking for someone to "help our customers make complex and important decisions." This probably would have helped 20 years ago if anyone had stopped to think about it.

The last thing to remember about millennials is that they are getting older. The median millennial is now 27 years old. That's hugely older than 23. Anything you figured out back in 2013 about dealing with 23-year-olds won't work with this year's 27-year-olds.

Since generational generalities are so hard, rely on Rule Number One: treat everyone as an individual.

Chapter 13

Leadership in a Tight Labor Market: Reduce Employee Turnover

Published on Forbes.com January 19, 2018

You have open positions to fill, and it's a tight labor market. Employees quit, but it's hard to hire. You need to get started recruiting to fill those empty positions, but wait – hiring should not be your top priority.

First you need to break the cycle of employee turnover. With vacant positions, your remaining employees are more stressed. Instead of helping those poor people, you're spending time covering for the workers who quit last week. Now your remaining employees are unhappy with the situation, and they are unhappy with the manager for ignoring them in such a difficult time. So another employee quits. And maybe another. And another.

Having two vacant positions is bad but here's what is worse: three vacant positions, or four. So first protect what you've got. Spend more time with your current employees.

Compensation has to be in the ballpark, but more people quit because of the manager than for pay. They may say they are quitting for more pay, but if they had a great manager, they never would have looked for more pay in the first place.

The best single strategy for employee retention is managerial attention. Tell the employees they are valuable. Offer feedback on how they are doing. Very few employees get enough feedback, and it really helps with retention. You can go ahead and give negative feedback too, so long as it comes with specific action steps for the employee to improve performance. Having a path to progress is positive, even if that path is based on fixing problems.

Senior leaders at large companies need to get their first-level supervisors talking to the rank and file employees. Unfortunately, those supervisors are already pretty busy: reports, compliance, handling customer complaints, and so forth. Adding additional work to an over-worked manager is a huge de-motivator and risks losing the manger, too.

The alternative is to tell the manager that the company is losing too many workers, and in this tight labor market it's hard to hire good people. Then say that the best solution is for managers to talk to employees more often, providing encouragement and offering feedback. Then ask the manager, "How can we free up time for you to do this?"

In today's tight labor market, companies need to shift resources to employee retention. Pay is one way to add resources to employee retention, but unless your compensation is below the competition, the better way is to put more management time into talking with employees.

Here's the challenge to getting this done: spending time with employees is a task without a deadline. The manager is thinking, "I need to get back to three customers by the end of the day, the compliance report is due on Friday, the conversion committee meets this afternoon." So any chore without a due date gets pushed off till next week. And then the week after. And then the week after that.

The challenge is even harder for managers who are not particularly extroverted: Talking to employees is not only a task without a deadline, it's outside of many managers' comfort zones. Reflect on that for a moment: how many tasks do you complete that lack deadlines and put you outside of your comfort zone?

Devoting more to time to employees means less time to *something else*. The company's leaders need to find that something else.

Increasing employee retention is the number one strategy for dealing with today's tight labor market. Add resources to the effort.

Chapter 14

New Evidence That Low Employee Turnover Correlates With High Profits

Published on Forbes.com April 19, 2018

Employee turnover is costly: the time and money spent hiring, the effort and distraction of training, the low productivity of new employees as well as reduced product quality or customer service while new employees come up to speed. I just saw hard evidence from a common industry: convenience stores/gasoline stations.

This is a huge industry, with 155,000 stores and 2.5 million employees. The industry's trade association, NACS, collects information from its members utilizing data feeds directly from accounting systems. They have hard numbers, not just opinions. And the hard numbers show that the most profitable stores have lower turnover of both managers and associates.

The data nerds divide convenience stores (mostly with gasoline pumps also) into quartiles based on store operating profit. Profit margin increases with dollar profits, so we can read this as profitability.

The top quartile stores had 75 percent turnover of associates per year, while the overall average was 115 percent.

I'm always skeptical of correlation interpreted as causation. It's possible that the most profitable stores can afford higher salaries, which leads to lower turnover. But the top quartile actually pay less per hour than the second quartile, and only a little more than the bottom quartile. Yet the top quartile has by far the best in-store gross profit per labor hour.

A more likely interpretation is that good management has many dimensions, with employee turnover being just one. Even if that's the case, note that turnover couldn't be better at the top stores unless management made it a priority.

Practical steps for reducing employee turnover were shown in a previous article, Leadership In Today's Tight Labor Market: Reduce Employee Turnover.

Resources:

NACS: http://www.convenience.org/

Hard numbers: https://www.convenience.org/Solutions/Store/pages/default.aspx?site=nacs_store&WebCode=storeCatList&catKey=cdc4da89-47c3-4cd0-9dec-4d9ac94f885d

Leadership In Today's Tight Labor Market: Reduce Employee Turnover: https://www.forbes.com/sites/billconerly/2018/01/19/leadership-in-a-tight-labor-market-reduce-employee-turnover/

Chapter 15

Promoting Wrong People Hurts Employee Retention And Productivity

Published on Forbes.com June 19, 2018

Managers are key to employee retention and productivity. But many companies don't promote into management the people who would do the best job as managers.

The importance of first level managers to employee retention is a conclusion confirmed by many research studies. Motivating and coaching staff members helps employee engagement, which boosts retention and productivity both. But this will be easier if the right people are in the job in the first place.

The most common promotion method is to move your best workers into management. That sometimes works, but not always. Remember the Peter Principle, that people rise to their level of incompetence? People are promoted until they no longer do a good job, and then they stay in that position—doing a poor job.

Now three economists (Alan Benson, Danielle Li and Kelly Shue) have found hard evidence. They looked at sales managers at over 200 companies and found that promoting the best sales people hurt future sales. Dipping into the ranks for the people best-suited to management produces stronger sales.

This is probably true in many other fields. My computer programmer friends tell me the top coders are often not the top managers. A great cop may not be a good supervisor of other police officers.

But there is a risk in NOT promoting your best workers—you'll discourage them. The possibility of promotion invents people to do their best.

So consider this strategy. First, look at your top-performing people and let them know they may be managers someday. Provide "pre-training" so they understand the person-to-person work needed. It's not just cracking the whip, as I'm sure you know—but maybe the workers don't know. The best managers tailor their conversations to the individual employee. Some people thrive on competition, while others freeze. Some are motivated by interesting work, while others enjoy routine. Good managers knows each direct report well enough to encourage in the best possible way.

Some great workers will say "I don't really want to spend my day understanding the motivations and worries of other people." It's fine if they take themselves out of the running.

Other great workers will take up the mantle of leadership, learn what they need to know, and succeed when they are promoted.

And if none of your top performers move up, they'll at least understand what the issue is when you promote a lower-ranked worker who has the skills to be a great manager.

But you still need to invent your best workers. Have a recognition system for excellence in work, both in job title and compensation, that provides an incentive without moving the person into management.

You may well end up with managers making less than some of their best workers. Nothing wrong with that. In some fields it's wasteful to have really talented workers spending their time scheduling shifts and arranging support services.

You need to look at your own organization and determine what traits great managers need to have, and how you can get the people with those traits into management. That will help employee retention as well as productivity.

Resources:

Alan Benson, Danielle Li and Kelly Shue:
http://www.nber.org/papers/w24343

Chapter 16

Retain More Employees With Stay Interviews

Published on Forbes.com July 21, 2018

Employees are quitting in droves, according to a recent Wall Street Journal article, backed up by hard data from the Bureau of Labor Statistics. Employee retention is easier than recruiting, I argued in my article about reducing employee turnover. And a great technique for employee retention is the Stay Interview.

Exit interviews are common but too much like talking to cows about why they left the barn. The stay interview asks why employees remain with you. The benefits are ample, argues Richard Finnegan, author of the cleverly titled book, The Stay Interview.

I spoke with Finnegan recently about the high quit rate across the economy. He said, "Hard data proves the top reason employees quit is they don't trust their managers. Stay Interviews are the absolute best trust-building activity…and therefore the best retention tool."

On the surface, the stay interview appears to be a mirror image to an exit interview, identifying things people like about their job rather than things they dislike. That's worthwhile, but the stay interview is much more valuable because it provides insights managers can use to motivate and retain the particular employee, not just a group.

Finnegan's recommended first question is what the employee looks forward to when coming to work. Aggregated, those answers may help you promote certain parts of the work experience. But aggregate answers gloss over what a particular employee looks forward to. If Alice likes facing new challenges, keep that in mind when tossing out work assignments. If it's novel, give it to Alice. There's probably another employee who looks forward to assignments that he has experience with.

Similarly, the question, "Why do you stay here?" can be aggregated while also providing the manager guidance for the specific employee. Something motivates the person to stay, and the more that the manager can reinforce and enhance that something, the longer the person will stay.

Sometimes the answer doesn't sound helpful, like, "I'm staying here for now, but my goal is to become a firefighter." I brainstormed that question with a group of convenience store managers, none of whom had an opening for a firefighter. But the group thought the manager could offer to be a reference source, including information about the employee's record showing up for shifts on time and following the company's safety policies. That transforms the position from a dead-end minimum wage job to a path to the employee's dream job. And it reinforces the value of showing up on time and following safety policies, worthwhile for all workers. But the manager only knows how to be helpful by talking to the employee.

Employee turnover projects often focus on broad themes: benefits, teamwork, company purpose. But each employee is unique. Each one has goals and dreads, hopes and fears, strengths and weaknesses. The managers with best retention performance work with each employee as an individual, customizing assignments, feedback and motivation to the individual worker. The Stay Interview is a great tool. Finnegan's book is a worthwhile explanation of the process.

Talking to employees comes naturally to some leaders, so a program of Stay Interviews may not seem necessary. However, for most managers talking to employees is a task without a deadline. And for some, it's a task without a deadline outside the manager's comfort zone! How good are any of us at tasks without deadlines outside our comfort zones?

Finnegan suggests going beyond the stay interview to a system that includes dollar impacts of turnover, goals, measurement and accountability. That's wise. It's too easy to bring in an idea, then have everyone forget it. Systems are good.

Whether a company uses stay interviews or some other method, getting managers talking to employees leads to better worker engagement and retention.

Resources:

Wall Street Journal: https://www.wsj.com/articles/in-this-economy-quitters-are-winning-1530702001?mod=searchresults&page=1&pos=8

Hard data from the Bureau of Labor Statistics: https://www.bls.gov/jlt/

About reducing employee turnover: https://www.forbes.com/sites/billconerly/2018/01/19/leadership-in-a-tight-labor-market-reduce-employee-turnover/#56c01c0a3a6a

The Stay Interview: https://www.amazon.com/Stay-Interview-Managers-Keeping-Brightest-ebook/dp/B00TRF2QA6/

Chapter 17

Companies Need To Know The Dollar Cost Of Employee Turnover

Published on Forbes.com August 12, 2018

I would roll my eyes when I heard that a company should know the cost of employee turnover. Okay, I thought, for a particular business the cost is $14.3 million. What would anyone ever do with that figure? It turns out that understanding turnover costs is critical for operations personnel as well as finance and human resources staff members.

As an economist, I want something a bit different from the total cost: How much would the cost increase if turnover worsened by one percentage point a year? How much would the cost fall if turnover were improved by one percentage point? Now we have data for a profit-maximizing decision: Would a particular change provide more value than it costs?

Turnover is generally considered bad, but McDonalds has built a business on high employee turnover. They have optimized their systems to train employees to do a good job and then leave in less than a year.

High turnover is not the right decision for every company, though. Costco believes that its low employee turnover is a great benefit.

Whichever strategy a business pursues, it should always be looking for cheap ways to improve turnover. Take the local McDonalds, good at training workers. A person with six months on the job is still more productive than someone is the first month of work. If McDonald's can get another month from its workers before they leave, then the productivity difference is huge.

Key to improving employee retention is knowing turnover costs. Before embarking on big programs, or even small programs, it's worth knowing how much benefit will accrue. Those cost estimates need to be owned by operations managers and finance. Operations people will implement the changes in first-level supervision that will produce results. To motivate them, costs need to be something they have worked to understand rather than figures given to them by outsiders. Finance personnel need to believe the numbers and support spending money that will save even more money in turnover costs.

Employee turnover is not just an issue for the human resources department. Operating units feel the pain of turnover in productivity, product quality and customer service. But the calculations are difficult, so finance personnel are probably best qualified. I suggest a team incorporating people from HR, finance and operations. Where there are many other people employed, like maybe a sales department, someone familiar with those activities should contribute to the effort.

Human resources costs are the tip of the iceberg, so let's look at them first. When an employee leaves, there's an exit interview and processing of the termination, including data to be entered into the benefits system.

Then the open position may be advertised, resumes reviewed and interviews arranged. In conjunction with the hiring manager, HR may work up an offer. HR or a training department may conduct an orientation training, along with enrollment in benefits programs. So far, these costs can be estimated fairly easily, especially if one doesn't expect an answer accurate to the penny.

The bigger part of the iceberg is outside of HR, in the work units where the new employee will land.

Before the new employee is hired, though, the open position will probably be covered by other employees, diverting them from their regular work or requiring overtime. Or activity is simply not done. If it's a sales position, that's a direct hit to the top line. Longer lead times on products could be costly as well. Throw in a bit of stress to the employees near the vacant seat.

Once the new worker is hired, there will be on-the-job training. The manager will spend time guiding and supervising the new person. Co-workers will probably help by answering questions, lowering their own productivity. And the new worker's productivity—both output and quality—will almost always be lower than that of experienced employees. Measuring these costs is difficult, but a clever analyst will come up with rough estimates. Don't expect perfection, and don't assign to the task a person who is overly precise—that's just not possible.

Thinking about these costs—productivity, supervision of new workers, and maintaining quality—points to the importance of operations people in the assessment. The complexity of the analysis points to having a good finance analyst on the team.

Off-the-shelf estimates are available, which might set the cost of an entry-level position turning over at 50 percent of salary; mid-level at

125 percent of salary; and senior executive over 200 percent of salary. There are also calculators that you can find online to help you with the arithmetic, including the well-known Bliss-Gately spreadsheet.

However you estimate your own costs, it's imperative that both operations and finance people come to own the estimate. They need to believe it is real. For the operations people, lower productivity and higher supervision costs are direct impacts on their performance. The finance people won't cheap-shot employee retention efforts when they have seen the real dollars and cents costs of employee turnover.

With the cost of turnover known, team leaders can survey possible turnover reductions and select those that most improve overall profits at the company.

Resources:

Bliss-Gately spreadsheet:
http://www.gatelyconsulting.com/PRCOSToT.htm

Chapter 18

Don't Delay That Performance Review

Published on Forbes.com March 2, 2019

Monday morning you see two reminders on your desk: to do an employee's performance review, and to schedule a root canal. Which one do you attend to first?

For many managers, it's a toss-up. Performance review and root canal seem equally bad. I've had a root canal, and it was actually painless, leading me to think that performance reviews should be done under Demerol.

But performance reviews are very valuable for employee retention. Job search activity by employees goes down around the time of performance reviews by 13% according to CEB analysis.

I recently discussed employee engagement, retention and productivity with a group of business leaders. I asked what they thought the impact of a performance review on employee retention was, and they expected a negative impact, which is not what the data show.

Why does a performance review improve employee retention? First, it shows the company's interest in an employee. The worker knows that it takes time and effort for the manager to do the performance review, and people appreciate that. Even though performance reviews are typically stressful for both participants, the review shows commitment to the employee. Postponing a performance review diminishes the employee's importance.

A good performance review gives the manager an opportunity to listen to the employee, to hear the person's motivations, hopes and dreams, and well as frustrations and fears. Sometimes the manager can do something helpful, but other times it's valuable just to listen. People want to be heard.

My favorite employee retention guru, Dick Finnegan of *The Stay Interview* fame, suggests a separate meeting to discuss why the employee chooses to remain on the job. That's good advice, but it usually does not happen in the absence of a clearly-defined program. The performance review becomes an easy way to get that conversation going.

Annual performance reviews have been abandoned at many companies and are hated or ignored at many others. A Harvard Business Review article by Peter Cappelli and Anna Tavis states, "With their heavy emphasis on financial rewards and punishments and their end-of-year structure, they hold people accountable for past behavior at the expense of improving current performance and grooming talent for the future, both of which are critical for organizations' long-term survival. In contrast, regular conversations about performance and development change the focus to building the workforce your organization needs to be competitive both today and years from now."

I have had success with frequent mini-reviews, as often of every two weeks, taking just five minutes or so each time. With continual feedback, the annual performance review has no surprises.

Abandoning annual performance reviews is only acceptable if they are replaced with another structure for feedback. Whether it's a weekly huddle or a quarterly conference, alternatives may work a little better or a little worse. A structured program to which managers are held accountable is necessary, or feedback stops for many employees. Talking to employees becomes a task without a deadline. Many people suck at tasks without deadlines.

And for some managers, talking about an employee's performance is outside of a the comfort zone. Hardly anyone is good at completing tasks without deadlines outside of their comfort zone.

A highly productive employee is highly engaged in the work and highly likely to stay with the company. That person knows what the boss thinks, both the good and the bad. The performance review facilitates that process, though it's not the only means of doing so.

Resources:

CEB analysis: http://www.cemla.org/actividades/2016/2016-04-RecursosHumanos/2016-04-RecursosHumanos4.pdf

Dick Finnegan: https://c-suiteanalytics.com/

Harvard Business Review article: https://hbr.org/2016/10/the-performance-management-revolution

Chapter 19

The Hardest Performance Reviews Are For Good Employees

Published on Forbes.com August 20, 2019

The hardest performance reviews are ones for good employees, not bad. Reviews for poorly performing employees may be unpleasant, but they are not hard to figure out. You identify what must change and explain that to the worker.

Good employees, though, often get performance reviews that make them want to leave. "Fred, you're doing a fine job. No complaints. Keep up the good work." How does that make Fred feel? Before answering, consider that movie. I don't recall the title, but the hero achieved what he wanted in the first 10 minutes, then spent the rest of the movie enjoying success. Did you see that movie? Actually, you didn't. Hollywood never made such a movie, because people don't want to achieve success and then enjoy it. People want progress. They want to overcome challenges.

In this example, Fred has nowhere to go. He's been told he is as good as he ever will be. It's nice he's not going to be fired, or even criticized, but that's not what the good performers want: They want a path to progress.

Managers must keep their best employees energized, which means seeking new goals. My fellow Forbes contributor Mark Murphy explained, "People with a high need for achievement seek to excel. Achievement-driven individuals thrive when they're allowed to stand out and be great .... They welcome constructive criticism ..." because it enables them to achieve at a higher level.

Unfortunately, good employees seldom get coaching about how to be even better employees. Providing some advice will re-energize your best employees, improving retention of those who are most productive and who set the best example for others.

Before the performance review, the best mangers consider how the person could do an even better job. Could he or she coach other employees who are not doing as well? Could the person anticipate problems better? Nobody is perfect, so some ideas should come to mind. When presenting the ideas, the top managers are positive. They say something like, "You're doing good work, on the path to great work. Let me give you some thoughts on what you could do to be the best worker ever." That's both praise and encouragement to improve.

What if nothing comes to mind? What if the manager has absolutely no idea how the employee could perform better at the particular job. A good boss then uses the performance review to brainstorm with the worker. "Sally, you're a great worker. But I'm torn. I think that nobody's perfect, that there is always room for improvement. But I don't have a clue what to tell you about being better at your job. So let's brainstorm."

The manager then brings up the broad categories in which improvement might fall.

In some jobs, production or sales can be increased. If that applies, the manager says "Do you have any ideas for boosting your output? Anything getting in the way of getting more done?"

In other jobs, costs might be open to improvement. "Do you have any ideas for how we can reduce our costs for what we are doing?"

In other positions, improving customer experience will be the most likely opportunity.

This conversation may bear fruit—or not. Brainstorming never results in predictable results. The process itself, though, brings the good employee into the discussion, gets the thought process going, and will probably lead the person to ponder the question off the job. The person's engagement in the job increases. Good workers will feel challenged to step up with ideas for improvement. Retention will improve.

Like all performance reviews, those for good employees require advance planning. With good preparation, the performance review will energize the good employee, leading to higher retention and productivity while inspiring other workers to emulate the example.

Resources:

Mark Murphy explained:
https://www.forbes.com/sites/markmurphy/2018/11/04/heres-why-you-still-need-to-conduct-performance-reviews-with-your-employees/#6c55eb5e19f8

Chapter 20

Hiring To Improve Employee Retention: Learning From Stay Interviews

Published on Forbes.com October 3, 2019

Employee retention will be the critical issue in the decade ahead as the labor market continues to tighten. (I explained the demographic trigger for this in my article, The Scariest Chart For Business In The Coming Decade: Workers Not Available.)

The best companies think about employee retention long before a new employee starts work. Recruiting for retention is a valuable element of an overall employee turnover strategy. It is easy for a manager to focus entirely on whether a candidate can do the job. Equally important is whether the candidate will want to do the job long enough to make the hire worthwhile.

The Stay Interview is a valuable employee retention technique, and the insights gained from multiple stay interviews give the manager the knowledge needed to hire new candidates who will choose to stay. Stay interviews are like exit interviews, but for employees who remain with the company. Exit interviews are like talking to cows who walked out of the barn when the door was left open. Stay interviews are like walking into the barn and asking the cows what they like about the barn and if they have ever thought about leaving.

Richard Finnegan, who wrote the book about stay interviews, recommends just five questions, starting with what the employee looks forward to when going to work, and ending with what could make the job better. A manager who has conducted stay interviews with all direct reports knows what the people like most about the job and least about the job. And that can help find the right person to add to the team.

For example, in some departments most people will say that the feature of the job they like best is constant interaction with co-workers to get the job done. In that department, the manager had better not hire a loner. If an applicant says in the job interview that the best part of the last job was working alone, then the person probably won't want to stay long on this job.

Many people look for cultural fit, and that's fine, but a bit too narrow. Within a corporation, there will be some teams in which the people interact with each other, and other teams of independent workers. Jobs will vary with respect to other work characteristics as well.

Job applicants can be understood by asking spectrum questions. For example, "Some people like to work on one task until it's completed, while others are happy being interrupted with urgent tasks that take priority. Obviously this is a spectrum, so tell me: where on the spectrum are you? Near the extreme of preferring one task at a time, near the opposite extreme of multi-tasking, or somewhere in the middle?" The usual answer is in the middle, so probe for middle shaded toward one end of the spectrum, or middle shaded toward the other end. The questions should be phrased in a neutral tone, so there's no implication that one end of the spectrum is better than another.

Other spectrum questions might be preference for high pressure or relaxed; detail-oriented or big picture; learning new techniques or sticking with established procedures. The hiring manager can review the stay interview responses to identify the characteristics that would best fit the team, then ask corresponding spectrum questions in interviews.

One exception to this retention strategy is if one job within a team needs a different personality. A sales department might have 10 sales reps and one person who coordinates scheduling with a production department. That one scheduler will have a different personality than the sales reps. In such an instance, the hiring manager can talk to colleagues in other departments who have more experience with that type of job and the personalities that fit the job well.

Other employee assessment tools, such as StrengthsFinder or Myers-Briggs, might be helpful but were not designed to determine job candidates most likely to stay. Of course, stay interviews are not designed for that purpose either, but they do indicate the top features of the job that people doing the job like, and the aspects of the job they would most like to change. Whatever tool the hiring manager uses, the essential goal is to hire people who will both do the job well, and who will choose to stay in the job.

Resources:

The Scariest Chart For Business In The Coming Decade: Workers Not Available: https://www.forbes.com/sites/billconerly/2018/03/25/the-scariest-chart-for-business-in-the-coming-decade-workers-not-available/#321caf633de9

Stay Interview:
https://www.forbes.com/sites/billconerly/2018/07/21/retain-more-employees-with-stay-interviews/

The book about stay interviews:
https://www.finneganinstitute.com/stay-interviews/

Chapter 21

Retaining And Recruiting Older Workers: Tight Labor Market Solution

Published on Forbes.com February 25, 2020

Retaining and even recruiting older workers will be a success strategy in the increasingly tight labor market for many companies. The economy is expanding, but with hardly any growth of the number of people of traditional working age. Higher productivity—more output per worker—won't go far enough to solve the labor supply problem. The best option available will be employing older workers.

Small gains in the employable population can come from more jobs for mothers of school-age children, and also from people who are currently discouraged or disabled. But the numbers in those categories, and the challenge of bringing them into the workforce, prevent them from solving the labor supply-demand mismatch. Only older workers are numerous enough and have the needed skills to keep American businesses growing in the next decade.

A new study by a team of economists from Vanguard, the Federal Reserve and several universities found that 60% of retired people are interested in going back to work if they can have flexible hours. And they are willing to accept a lower pay rate than they earned in their career jobs. The group studied were Vanguard customers, who average higher incomes and wealth than the general population. These results probably don't extend to occupations with significant physical activity.

The respondents' careers were concentrated in management, professional/technical services and education.

Even though this study result may not apply to all positions, it warrants consideration for many open jobs. Flexible hours, in this study, means the ability to choose the number of hours worked per week, or the number of weeks per year. Details of flexibility would need to be worked out by any company looking at their options. Some companies could easily handle the senior worker who wants to spend six weeks in Florida in the winter, and others could handle the senior who doesn't want to commute at rush hour. The most successful companies will consider just what flexibility they can accommodate, and what aspects of the work must be fixed. When the business needs a person available to help a customer from 8 to 5, then flexible options may be limited.

Worker productivity may be lower with flexible schedules, an issue that the best companies will think through ahead of time. The time needed to understand company policies and procedures is an overhead for each employee, and it will be the same overhead whether the employee works 10 hours a week or 40.

Businesses must also consider how senior workers on a flexible schedule relate to younger workers on a fixed schedule. Resentment is possible, so clarification of the deal will be helpful.

Flexibility can even be offered across the board. Many millennials believe that they would be more productive if they could work flexible hours, according to a study by Bentley University researchers. When flexibility will be difficult for the company (such as when a function must be covered during certain hours), two pay scales could be offered: flexible schedules would pay less than fixed schedules. Everyone on the team would understand that flexibility is a choice, and there's no need to resent another worker's choice.

Making work more appealing to seniors will be a key success tool for businesses in the tight labor market, but implementing flexibility will take some trial and error. The top performing companies a decade from now will be those that figured it out.

Resources:

A new study:
https://pubs.aeaweb.org/doi/pdfplus/10.1257/mac.20170403

A study by Bentley University researchers:
https://www.bentley.edu/news/new-survey-reveals-what-millennials-really-think-about-work

American Economic Journal: Macroeconomics 2020, 12(1): 174–209
https://doi.org/10.1257/mac.20170403

Older Americans Would Work Longer if Jobs Were Flexible:
https://pubs.aeaweb.org/doi/pdfplus/10.1257/mac.20170403

Chapter 22

Tolerating Low Performance Employees In A Tight Labor Market

Published on Forbes.com January 19, 2022

Business leaders know that tolerating poor performance by employees is bad practice. But today's labor market is so tight that replacing an employee is very difficult. What is a manager to do with poor workers? There's no pat answer applicable across the board, but there are several key issues to consider.

Remember why tolerance of poor employees is bad. First, the employee does poor work, but that is the least of the problems. Other workers see the poor performer coming to work and collecting a paycheck. Nobody feels motivated. And other workers often have to cover for the worker who comes in late, does the job poorly or finishes too little productive activity. The poor performing employee causes low motivation and low morale of all the nearby workers.

The low performing employee also sucks up too much of the manager's time. The 80-20 rule may also apply to management, according to leadership coach David Rabiner: 80% of the manager's time is taken up by 20% of the employees. And which 20% of employees get the attention? Hint: it's not the top performers. Could the operation be improved if the manager spent more time recognizing the top performers and encouraging them to stay with the company? Would it help if the manager spent more time coaching the moderate performers to be better? Is the manager spending enough time talking to customers and planning for improvements in efficiency? The worst employees divert the manager's time and energy from growth to damage control. And a business's scarcest resource is the time of its leaders.

But before firing a low performing employee, the manager will contemplate how to find a replacement. That's certainly a challenge. Unemployment is low, unfilled positions abound, radio stations play help-wanted commercials and nearly every business displays a "Now Hiring" sign.

The decision process must cover both short-run issues and long-run company performance. The short-run issue begins with whether the person needs to be replaced at all. Although usually the case, it's not always true. When recessions force cost cutting, many companies are able to cut both production workers and administrative staff. Businesses often find that they can still get the work done with fewer employees.

Today, however, most companies run lean, not fat. Managers have seen departures and been unable to hire, so little slack is left.

In situations where people have narrowly defined jobs, the manager knows the impact of a departure. In many cases, especially in smaller businesses or departments, people have accumulated multiple responsibilities. A person may, for example, be primarily an accounts payable clerk, but also help out with ordering or payroll. The manager wonders how to find someone who can handle all of those tasks. The bright side reflects that the person probably grew into the role organically, with additional tasks added over time. So the manager might focus on finding someone to do the primary task while reallocating the other responsibilities to other employees.

Another short-term consideration in dismissing a low performing employee is whether other workers are likely to quit because of the poor performer. The other workers have options in this economy. If the problem employee is disruptive or angers other employees, then firing the person may retain the other workers. The decision becomes simpler: Who would the manager rather keep, the disruptive employee or the nearby workers who are unhappy with the disruptive person?

The long-term question for the manager faced with a low performing employee is what kind of company culture to emphasize. Company culture comes not from the platitudes on posters in the break room but from the daily decisions that business leaders make. If the daily decisions tolerate low performance, than the company culture becomes "just get by." But if daily decisions emphasize higher productivity, then most staff members step up to do their best work. People who enjoy doing good work stay, and the slackers either don't apply for jobs there or they leave of their own volition pretty soon.

A manager can be supportive of people with temporary setbacks because of health or personal issues without weakening a high-performance culture. Employees understand that their colleagues go through times of trouble. But when workers take advantage of the manager's kindly nature to malinger or disrupt operations, the entire business is threatened.

Dismissing a low performer is difficult, the worst task for most managers. But even in this tight job market, it's a task that must be done.

Resources:

David Rabiner: https://rabiner.com/about/

Chapter 23

Employee Retention Through Training Opportunities

Published on Forbes.com October 17, 2022

A business owner sent this note to new employees:

> "I'm writing to let you know that [the company] wants to provide a path for you to be successful with our company. You will not find another company that is willing to provide you the opportunity and training to be successful and go as far as you want to go. Please make an appointment to come meet with me on most Saturdays. Sometimes, I also work on Sundays. We can discuss a path for improvement. It is very simple to understand and achieve if you are willing to do it."

In a tight labor market, recruiting and retaining good employees is tough but vital. Upgrading the skills of existing employees is often easier than trying to go out and recruit experienced and talented workers. And the best workers will read the note and want to continue working at the company because the owner is trying to help employees. This attitude is far more valuable for employee retention than yoga classes and other frills.

The business owner is Manuel Castaneda of PLI Systems, a soil stabilization contractor in Hillsboro, Oregon. (He and I serve together on the board of directors of Cascade Policy Institute.) Castaneda came to this country as a teenager unable to speak English. He started a lawn mowing service while in high school. In 1989 he learned how to operate construction equipment on steep surfaces to mitigate landslides and started his current company. He has 44 employees.

Asked the motivation for his note, Castaneda said that his employees may see opportunities to make a dollar or two more somewhere else. He wanted them to know that they could do much better by staying with the company and upgrading their skills.

Tips for employees followed the lead paragraph. For example, "A CDL [commercial drivers license] gives you the freedom to be more independent. Once you know how to do the work and use equipment, you can move your own equipment and not be dependent on someone else. This allows you to grow much quicker." He followed that tip with this comment: "If you can't get your CDL now because you made mistakes in the past, don't worry. Start training and learning other skills that don't require driving for now. Eventually, time will pass and you will be ready when the opportunity presents. Just don't do dumb things again to be suspended."

Other tips were straightforward: "Learn how to read plans. We provide classes for plan reading. Just let me know and we can make it happen." This offer was made to entry level laborers who had no current need to read plans, but for whom the skill would be valuable in taking on more responsibility.

In the first two weeks, half of the new employees made appointments to talk to the owner.

The company helps owners of buildings on steep hillsides or with drainage challenges. That's not solving all of the world's problems, but it's solving specific problems faced by specific people. Castaneda doesn't brag to employees about saving the world. Instead he offers them a path to gain pay, responsibility and respect. The workers probably start out thinking about more pay, but earning the pay comes from being worthy of more responsibility, and the result is not only pay but also more respect—both self-respect and the respect of others.

Every CEO is a sales person, and part of the role is sell jobs to current and prospective employees. Sales people are coached to emphasize the benefits of their product to customers. In today's labor market, an employee doesn't have to buy a job from you; he or she can get a job most anywhere. So the CEO's pitch to employees, both for retention and recruiting, must include what's in it for the employee. Notes such as this one focus on potential benefits.

Castaneda concluded the letter with a final piece of advice: "Find habits that help you improve your life and think of a brighter future." That's good advice for anyone.

Part 5

Improving Labor Recruiting

Chapter 24

Hiring In A Tight Labor Market: 6 Tips For A Busy Manager

Published on Forbes.com May 24, 2017

Even a short trip down the street reveals multiple signs: "Help Wanted," "Now Hiring," "Applications Being Accepted." Hiring workers in a tight labor market is more work for managers than it used to be. Employee retention is always a higher priority than employee recruiting, as I wrote in "Quits Are Up: 7 Employee Retention Strategies Your Company Must Have." But retention isn't enough; you also need to find workers to replace those who do leave and for expansion.

1. **Use all the available tools**. This is advice I give to job seekers all the time. They often focus too narrowly on online job boards. Similarly, some managers put all of their effort into one channel. Instead, consider all recruiting tools: Help Wanted signs outside your business, online job posts, referrals from current employees, and general networking.

2. **Look for untapped reservoirs of people**. The overall unemployment rate is a low 4.4 percent (as of April 2017), but that average masks higher unemployment rates for certain groups: teenagers, African Americans, Native Americans and those without a high school diploma. Sometimes an employer does not have the flexibility to look into these groups. You will not find a registered nurse among those without a high school diploma, nor an accountant with a CPA ticket among teenagers. But make sure that your recruiting efforts are aligned with the untapped reservoirs that are available to you. If you could use more teenagers, for example, talk to your current teenaged employees about the best way to find other teenagers.

Rural areas typically have higher unemployment rates than urban areas. That will not help you if your business is located in Manhattan, but if your company is in a suburban area, then perhaps you can recruit from a neighboring rural county.

Unemployment among immigrants is relatively low, but there may be good opportunity's among the most recent arrivals. Check to see if your community has a service center for refugees or other recent immigrants.

Veterans have a slightly higher-than-average unemployment rate, and the Department of Labor can help employers find qualified veterans.

3. **Consider the long-term unemployed**. Many people became discouraged when jobs were hard to find during the recession. These people would have found jobs in a normal economic environment and would have been considered desirable employees. They often became discouraged or found opportunities outside of formal employment. Now their resumes make them look like damaged goods to some employers. That

is understandable when employers can be particular, but not when workers are hard to find. Give them a try.

4. **Reconsider your minimum requirements**. When job applicants are abundant, it's easy to look for more education, more experience, and a more pleasant personality. Now it is time to reconsider the job requirements. Does the person really need the degree or diploma or certification that you have required? For every job opening, look at every requirement and think about whether it is absolutely necessary.

Easing requirements is best done in stages. Instead of loosening all requirements at once, take a guess at the one requirement that, if eased, could get you the most quality applicants. Try that one, and see how it works. If you change multiple criteria at once, it will be difficult to tell where you went right and where you went wrong.

5. **Ask your customers**. Your customers already have an understanding of your business. Some of them may be looking for work. (This is more of a B-C strategy than a B-B strategy, because you probably do not want your customers to think that you're poaching their employees.) Your customers may also be referral sources for new employees. So if you have a newsletter or regular e-mail or advertising flyer, mention that you are hiring.

6. **Keep your eyes open for great workers**. A friend of mine was shopping for clothes and got great service from a sales representative. She asked the saleswoman, "Have you ever thought of working at a bank? You would be great at it, and you would not have to work evenings and weekends." The saleswoman asked if the customer knew anybody at a bank. The

customer chuckled and said, “Yes I do,” then handed her a business card. She was president of a bank.

The hiring challenge will be with us for a while, driven partly by recent economic growth as well by long-term trends: baby boomers retiring and a relatively small generation entering the workforce in the wake of the Millennials. For your business to thrive, the challenge of a tight labor market must be addressed immediately.

Resources:

Quits Are Up: 7 Employee Retention Strategies Your Company Must Have: https://www.forbes.com/sites/billconerly/2013/12/11/quits-are-up-7-employee-retention-strategies-your-company-must-have/#5b4e2d0b7ed4

Unemployment among immigrants: https://www.bls.gov/news.release/forbrn.nr0.htm

Veterans: https://www.bls.gov/news.release/vet.nr0.htm

Department of Labor: https://www.dol.gov/veterans/employers/local.htm

Chapter 25

Three Steps To Hire With Lower Education Requirements: Successfully Coping With The Tight Labor Market

Published on Forbes.com February 25, 2018

It's time to rethink the qualifications you require in a job applicant. That diploma has value, but there are ways to find good candidates without diplomas.

The tight job market is translating into companies having trouble finding qualified applicants for open positions. DHI Hiring Indicators shows much longer time to fill job vacancies now compared to even the pre-recession boom. Economists at The Conference Board see employment growth for people without diplomas, both no-college and even no-high school.

Also influencing people is an important new book by Bryan Caplan, The Case Against Education. Caplan says:

While the labor market rewards good grades and fancy degrees, most of the subjects schools require simply aren't relevant on the job. Literacy and numeracy are vital, but few of us use history, poetry, higher mathematics or foreign languages after graduation. The main reason firms reward education is because it certifies (or "signals") brains, work ethic and conformity.

When labor is abundant, requiring a diploma is an easy way to separate wheat from chaff. It isn't a perfect way, but it's easy to administer. For example, a particular job may not require the skills of a college grad who majored in Russian literature, but that grad certainly has brains, persistence and tolerance for BS. But with very low unemployment, it may be time to relax those standards.

What will you, the employer, get if you hire the college dropout rather than college grad, or high school dropout rather than high school grad? You'll probably get less of those three signaling elements: brains, work ethic and conformity. Here's how to work through the issues.

1. **Brains**: If the job requires pretty smart people, look for other evidence of brains. The person admitted to a top university is certainly smart, even if he or she dropped out. With other candidates, you can look for indicators of brains from previous jobs the person has held or from hobbies.
2. **Persistence**: is, in my experience, the biggest difference between completion and non-completion of degrees. I consider my own degrees a tribute not to my brains but to my damn-fool stubbornness. In a highly supervised work environment, you don't need to worry so much about persistence. Where people work independently, though, this is a vital attribute. Look for candidates who can demonstrate persistence or grit another way, such as through a previous job, volunteer activity or an outside interest. Keep in mind that many young people are not ready to sit down and study at age 16 or 20. That's especially true of males. But with some maturity, even men buckle down and work.
3. **Conformity**: Finally, the graduate demonstrates a tolerance for following rules or putting up with BS. Schools are full of silly rules, arbitrary requirements, and process-oriented standards that serve the bureaucracy of education but add little to the student's knowledge or skills. If your company has lots of rules, you probably need the signaling that comes from the diploma. When I'm in the hospital, I want a nurse who follows the rules. I've toured factories that use dangerous chemicals; those are good places for rules followers. But I've also seen companies that keep rules long after they have lost their reasons for existence or for trivial bookkeeping convenience. If this is your company, first go into full Trump mode and cut 22 regulations

> for every new one issued. (And if you don't really cut 22 regulations, just say you did to make the point.) If you can't cut the rules, because of safety requirements, you probably need to keep hiring graduates.

There's no one answer for every company, but any business having trouble finding talent in today's tight labor market should consider easing back on degree requirements. However, never cut back on the core values that drive your organization. That might be honesty, respect for customers, or a safety concern. Watch my YouTube video to learn more about the need to hire for core values.

Resources:

DHI Hiring Indicators: http://dhihiringindicators.com/

The Conference Board: https://www.conference-board.org/blog/postdetail.cfm?post=6706&blogid=7&mkt_tok=eyJpIjoiWVdZMk1qY3pOVFpoT1RGaSIsInQiOiJ1SW1cL2VaMU1mVTlhOFE5OXRDTXhnelwvUnZ3bk01MVByT2k1eFVwZ3AzYWhsTWtQVWpvYjJ4eWd1WTF5RzNsUGJBMGhYNCtSdHZcL2Z5VUtjRVhOS1VybWFxVVBwdTB5TkxCelVubFppdTdJaUF6QjFvdWdubFwvd2VsZmFlQTZhRWMifQ==

The Case Against Education: https://www.amazon.com/Case-against-Education-System-Waste/dp/0691174652

Caplan says: http://www.latimes.com/opinion/op-ed/la-oe-caplan-education-credentials-20180211-story.html

Need to hire for core values:
https://www.youtube.com/watch?v=LV5vTkDADwQ

Chapter 26

How To Find Employees From Businesses That Are Cutting Back

Published on Forbes.com November 18, 2018

Layoffs are always happening, even in a strong economy. Some industries are downsizing even though most of the economy is hopping. This offers hope for short-staffed employers: look for the downsizing sectors and recruit their employees.

This idea is evergreen but illustrated by a current sector in decline: home sales.

Right now, rising mortgage rates are hurting home sales. Sales of new homes are down 13.2% from a year ago. Sales of existing homes have declined 4.1% over the past 12 months. And mortgage rates have increased by just over one percentage point in the past year, so very few people are refinancing their mortgages. This is not a disaster, but it means that the home sales sector doesn't need as many employees as it formerly did. Layoffs have already begun, and more are likely.

I've spoken with a title insurance manager who is trimming staff. Mortgage brokers are likely to be downsizing. Real estate brokerages may also run leaner. Normal attrition may prevent layoffs in some cases, but in other companies layoffs are necessary.

The hiring manager has two challenges: how to find industries downsizing, and how to find employees who are now available.

For industries downsizing in the United States, go to the Bureau of Labor Statistics table Current Employment Statistics. As I am writing, I see downsizing in some manufacturing sectors such as printing, some types of retail stores such as sporting goods, and some service sectors such as advertising. Also, keep your ears open for companies having difficulties. Even in strong sectors, there will be a company or two that is in trouble.

For finding people who may now be available, reach out to anyone you know in the downsizing sectors. Nobody may come to mind right away, but use Facebook and LinkedIn to remind yourself of who you know. In LinkedIn's search box, where you would normally enter a person's name or a specific company, you can enter an occupation (mortgage broker) or a company type (title insurance) and find contacts that fit your search. You don't have to find unemployed people, just someone in the industry who knows other people in the industry. Shoot out a brief email mentioning that you're hiring and would appreciate any referrals they can offer.

Finding specialized skills will be difficult with this method, but for salespeople or office staff, it's better than another "Now Hiring" sign in the window.

We don't wish a weak economy on anyone, but change is inevitable. You will be doing those laid-off workers a service if you reach out and find them right away.

Resources:

Sales of new homes:
https://www.census.gov/construction/nrs/pdf/newressales.pdf

Sales of existing homes: https://www.nar.realtor/newsroom/existing-home-sales-decline-across-the-country-in-september

Mortgage rates: https://fred.stlouisfed.org/graph/?g=m1Ua

Current Employment Statistics:
https://www.bls.gov/web/empsit/ceseeb1a.htm

Chapter 27

Competing For Employees With Google, Amazon And The Other Tech Giants

Published on Forbes.com December 19, 2018

How does an employer compete for employees against the tech giants? Facebook, Microsoft and the rest can pay extremely high salaries for top employees. They even pay high salaries for non-programmers. More than one executive in the Seattle area has told me that hiring someone with basic Excel skills is tough, given Amazon's high demand for people. The answer is to try to avoid the tech giants as much as possible.

This article addresses two issues: programming talent and other people, including analysts, marketers and the like.

For programmers, the received wisdom of tech was described by Joel Spolsky, the co-founder of Fog Creek Software: "In our field, the top 1 percent of the workforce can easily be 10 times as productive as the average developer. The best developers invent new products, figure out shortcuts that save months of work, and, when there are no shortcuts, plow through coding tasks like a monster truck at a tea party."

If you really want the top one percent, there's a standard formula based on recruiters identifying talent in their early years of college, offering summer jobs and nursing relationships. The executive time that goes into recruitment adds costs on top of the high salaries and signing bonuses that these programmers can command. Is there a better way?

Ask yourself just how much talent you really need. Many of your programmers may be doing moderately mundane work most of the time. If you will have people doing less-than-revolutionary coding, then lower your sights to mid-quality programmers.

In Silicon Valley, even lower-quality programmers will be expensive. Instead, consider locating a shop in a university town. Places like Madison or Tucson might enable you to find locally-educated people who have put down roots next to their schools. If your location is inflexible, try recruiting out to the second-tier computer science programs. The top students at a second-tier college are probably as good as an M.I.T. student, though there won't be as many of them. Also get in touch with small liberal arts colleges, which are often ignored by companies recruiting on a large scale.

For non-programming talent, try to move away from the tech giants. One Seattle executive whose company had acquired another business refused to do the usual cost-cutting steps: consolidating back-office operations at headquarters. Instead, he invited his corporate employees to move to the smaller city where the acquisition was located. Many of those people liked the affordability and small-city atmosphere in the other location. In this case, nobody was forced to relocate, but the parent company's growth was all at the smaller city. Great workers wanted to get away from the crowded big city.

Thinking outside the box is a trite phrase, but good advice when competing for talent against highly profitable tech behemoths.

Brainstorm options, talk to your employees about why they stay on the job, and try cheap and easy tests of different strategies. And shoot me an email about what works for you.

Resources:

Described by Joel Spolsky:
https://www.inc.com/magazine/20070501/column-guest.html

Why they stay on the job:
https://www.forbes.com/sites/billconerly/2018/07/21/retain-more-employees-with-stay-interviews/#37861a2df18c

Chapter 28

Hiring Young Workers Who Want Work-Life Balance: What's An Employer To Do?

Published on Forbes.com January 14, 2019

"Millennials and Gen Z don't want to work long hours," I hear older managers complain. "They want work-life balance. When I was their age, I put in the time needed to get the job done."

What are we to do with these kids? We need the workers, but can we achieve our business goals with them?

The good news is that there are plenty of great workers among millennials and Gen Z. More good news: thinking through these issues can help your business improve employee engagement and lower staff turnover rates. But the bad news: you may have to change some of your behavior.

The facts about young workers are clear. There are about 60 million millennials. There are a few million in Gen Z now working and millions more soon to enter the work force. Do you think there are 60 million identical people? The wide diversity among the group is more important than the generalizations. Sure, some are slackers, but some are hard workers. Some want work-life balance, but others want a job they can throw themselves into. As I said in an earlier article, The Number One Rule For Dealing With Millennials In The Workplace is to treat everyone as an individual.

The generalizations about young people have a little truth, kind of like tall people have an easier time playing basketball. But although that generalization is true, we've all seen exceptions: clumsy tall people and athletic short guys with great moves.

Begin with what your company really needs. Maybe your starting workers toil very long hours, as in investment banking or law or medicine. Do you really need that, or is it just a traditional rite of passage?

If you have to make a choice, weigh carefully what you'll get from a requirement of long hours of hard work, versus an environment of a fair day's work for a fair day's pay. You can certainly find people willing to put in long hours—for a high price—but you might get a better deal by offering more livable terms of work. That would certainly broaden the range of people you could hire and reduce turnover in the first years of employment.

But do you really have to make a choice? Remember that some young people want work-life balance, while others want to throw themselves into a job. You can hire both types of people, if you structure the reward system right. Some tech companies, for example, pay a salary based on moderate hours, plus a bonus based on production. The people who sweat and strain—or the programming equivalent—get high rewards. The less-ambitious people know that they have not qualified for the top bonuses, but they also know they had their evenings and weekends free.

To have both types of people working together, measuring output is vital. Too often businesses measure input: how many hours were worked. But we all know of unproductive hours, and we sometimes see highly effective people working slacker hours and delivering workaholic results.

If a business cannot measure output well enough for differential compensation, then it must choose: demand long hours or ask for moderate hours. Either choice is viable, though they will cost different amounts per worker. It's a joke to expect long hours and extreme commitment from people who are paid as if they just phone it in. Perhaps that was possible once, long ago. More likely, just a few ambitious people took the low-wage jobs. They showed such great effort that they got promoted. Now they are managers wondering why not everyone is like themselves.

Resources:

The Number One Rule For Dealing With Millennials In The Workplace: https://www.forbes.com/sites/billconerly/2017/12/27/rule-number-one-for-dealing-with-millennials-in-the-workplace/#1113af35c6fc

Chapter 29

Why You Should Hire Video Game Players

Published on Forbes.com May 23, 2019

Many people of my generation have little respect for video game players, and this applies to job interviews. We might respect an applicant who plays competitive bridge or chess, but video games? No way.

My own children have helped me see more respect for the pastime. One of my sons came off of a game talking about his challenges: “I was getting ready for an attack, but first I wanted to make an investment of resources in a mine, which would give me more resources in future turns. But then I got attacked from the south. I had to deal with that, while still trying to build future resources. And the guy I had an alliance with to the west started acting like he might sever our relationship. But I still saw the opportunity for that attack I was planning. I had too many priorities, and they were all urgent. I needed to prepare for the future, but also defend myself today. It was harrowing.”

Does that sound like a job to you? It certainly does to me. The simplest games may seem to be all about reflexes and aim, but many modern games have economic challenges. Resources today, or resources for the future, is a fundamental issue of humankind. Hunters-gatherers decided whether to build tools that would ease future work burdens. The industrial revolution was built on capital that could have been spent on current consumption. Corporations today can invest in research and development to bring new technologies into production, or they can buy back more stock to boost shareholders' current income.

Fortnight: Battle Royale is one of the most popular games these days, and The Guardian has a parents' guide to the game. Players start on an island where they must find weapons, but they must also explore the territory. They can find one weapon and use it, or they can try to delay conflict until they have found better weapons. They can use resources to build defensive structures, or go on the attack right away. Choices, choices, choices.

One version of the game has players in teams. People are getting together with their friends to work together. Inevitably, they must reach a group consensus about the best strategy to employ. There will be differences of opinion. Some players will want to be cowboys while still part of the team, while others will want all team members to align their activities to the group strategy. Anyone ever been in a corporate meeting?

Businesses are starting to see the value of video game experience, as the *Wall Street Journal* recently wrote. One manager said that his company was looking for "trainability," and that gamers had usually learned not just one game, but dozens. They knew that each game had its own rules, which must be learned. The strategy that works best in one game may not work in another, so players have to evaluate their own work to see if they are on the most effective path. Ever see employees grumble that software forces them to work differently than they used to?

Job candidates should do more than say they play games. They should "provide context and evidence-based stories that can demonstrate why their gaming experience is valuable," according to Cori Bernosky, a human resources executive quoted by the *Wall Street Journal*. Interviewers should be ready to draw out gamers, asking about things such as cooperation, evaluation of strategies, when to shift paradigms, and so forth. Some games do fit the old stereotype of simply reflecting aim and reflexes, so probe about the type of gaming the job candidate likes.

One key ingredient in business success is persistence, or grit. Some gamers clearly have this, as shown by high ambition and long work to achieve those high goals.

Earning a 4.0 grade point average can usually be accomplished with a single strategy. Winning at multiple games will require multiple strategies, along with the same diligence exhibited by those honor role students. The gamer job applicants might turn out to be much better employees than older managers now imagine.

Resources:

Fortnite: Battle Royale: https://www.theguardian.com/games/2018/mar/07/fortnite-battle-royale-parents-guide-video-game-multiplayer-shooter

Wall Street Journal: https://www.wsj.com/articles/when-a-passion-for-videogames-helps-land-that-job-11551888001?mod=searchresults&page=1&pos=1

Guardian has a parents' guide: https://www.theguardian.com/games/2018/mar/07/fortnite-battle-royale-parents-guide-video-game-multiplayer-shooter

The Wall Street Journal recently wrote: https://www.wsj.com/articles/when-a-passion-for-videogames-helps-land-that-job-11551888001?mod=searchresults&page=1&pos=1

Chapter 30

Hiring Job Applicants You Previously Rejected

Published on Forbes.com July 24, 2019

I sifted through dozens to resumes and invited the top three applicants in for interviews. One was not suitable, but the other two seemed fine. I offered the position to the one with more relevant experience, and she accepted. Problem solved. For about a month.

My new hire told me that her father, who lived in another state, had just had a severe health crisis. She was going to move to help him. She appreciated my confidence in her but could not work for me.

Other people have had this experience with slightly different reasons. Health problems, marriage, divorce, another job offer, spouse is taking a job out of town, or the new hire just doesn't like the job. To make the problem worse, plenty of managers have had to fire new hires. They didn't show up, fell asleep on the job, stole money, didn't have the skills they claimed, and so forth.

When one new hire doesn't work out, there is no need to start over. In my case, I called applicant number two, explained what had happened and offered her the job. She accepted it and did a great job. But it may not be easy to get a rejected candidate to accept an offer later. Planning ahead for this contingency will help.

Contact rejected applicants, especially those you've interviewed, as soon as your top candidate accepts the job. This would seem to be common courtesy, but Wall Street Journal columnist Sue Shellenbarger reports, "A growing number of job applicants are being ghosted—interviewing for jobs, then getting no follow-up response from the employer."

Treating applicants well, by reporting to them your status, is an important step to building their confidence. Just telling them that the position was filled is nice. A little positive feedback will also build the relationship. That's easy to do by praising the applicant and reporting why you chose someone else. "I was impressed by your qualifications, but we offered the position to someone with more experience." Or someone stronger in programming. Or someone with expertise in video editing. Every hiring decision is based on multiple dimensions, so it's easy to be honest.

Many hiring managers don't want to risk an uncomfortable conversation, though much of the communication can be done by email.

If the rejected candidate does reach the manager by telephone or in person, it's wise to have a strategy. The simplest is to not get engaged in an argument about the candidate's qualifications. A simple statement that the decision has been made should be adequate.

However, a wise job-seeker would ask politely, "What would have made me a stronger candidate?" Pick an element that is fixable. Saying, "You are not smart enough for this job" doesn't help the candidate. Saying that knowledge of diesel engines would be useful gives the person something to work on.

For those candidates who were not interviewed (neither by phone nor in person), a response to an application is an unexpected bonus. It's very easy to do with an email. If you have to go back and sift through the resumes a second time, having built some good will can be valuable.

Senior level executives should expect their first-level managers to adhere to these guidelines, for two reasons. First, a hiring manager who won't have an uncomfortable communication with a job applicant won't have one with an employee, either. The discipline of communicating with applicants will train the manager to talk to employees more often, which is critical to good employee performance and retention.

The second reason managers should communicate with applicants is company reputation. Job applicants hear about a company, not a manager. When one manager is rude—such as ignoring a candidate after an interview—the entire company is considered rude.

Employee recruiting is difficult in today's tight labor market. The simple practice of treating people nicely will go a long way toward finding and keeping good workers.

Resources:

Wall Street Journal: https://www.wsj.com/articles/job-interview-etiquette-isnt-just-for-the-applicants-11562578204

Sue Shellenbarger reports: mailto: https%3A//www.wsj.com/articles/job-interview-etiquette-isnt-just-for-the-applicants-11562578204

Chapter 31

Labor Shortage Strategy: Rethink Job Requirements

Published on Forbes.com April 12, 2022

The extremely tight labor market is easing—just a bit—but will remain tighter than in the past decade through at least 2030. Businesses trying to hire workers will need to be creative, and one element of a good employment strategy is to rethink requirements for the jobs.

The labor market will not return to the "good old days" when job applicants were abundant. The demographics just don't work. Baby boomers are retiring, and the young people entering their working-age years are not larger in number. Foreign immigration is very low and unlikely to increase. Companies should be certain that their job requirements are necessary for high productivity, or try abandoning those rules.

The employee retention expert Dick Finnegan wrote, "Stop posting higher-level, impractical job requirements that screen out applicants who can do your job…and that also invite over-qualified applicants who will become bored with your job and quit." The first half of that sentence aims at recruiting, and the second half highlights that good employee retention starts with good hiring.

The first common job requirement to be reconsidered is education. Certainly you want your brain surgeon to have an M.D. degree, but do your sales manager, IT tech and purchasing manager need undergraduate degrees? Does your shipping clerk need a high school diploma?

The Case Against Education argues that education does not teach skills so much as signal to employers that the graduate has some combination of brains, persistence and conformity to rules. The author, Bryan Caplan, cites recent data and studies, but his 2018 book continues a hypothesis that is at least 50 years old. A competitive advantage will accrue to any employer who can find undervalued assets: people who lack the credential but can do the work.

Note that the simple correlations between college education and career success do not control for intelligence, persistence and conformity. And that conformity factor did not seem to be an issue in the success of famous dropouts such as Bill Gates, Steve Jobs and Mark Zuckerberg.

A business owner read Caplan's book and abandoned the college requirement for software coders. According to a recent letter to Caplan, the company explicitly welcomed non-degreed applicants, substituting tests for diplomas. Passing a job-specific test shows the applicant has the necessary brains. Persistence or "grit" is harder to measure in tests, but a candidate's history provides evidence. A person who dropped out of school to sit on a beach may not be a good hire. But a person who pursued a goal, even if unsuccessfully, may show the needed persistence. As for willingness to put up with stupid rules, a college diploma ensures that personality trait—but the employer should eliminate the stupid rules rather than hire people who won't object to them.

Experience requirements should also be reconsidered. Rather than years in a similar type of job, list the essential skills needed. Then consider how to evaluate applicants for those specific skills. Some people with experience do not have all the skills assumed, and others with less experience will have the necessary skills. Even if applicants were available in abundance, testing for specifics will be more successful than assuming that experience equates to skill.

For positions where the company really needs to hire experienced people, it's worth asking how much experience. An old saw states that 20 years of experience might be one year of experience repeated 20 times. Given the uncertainty, an experiment could help. A business that has always had a requirement for two years' experience for a certain position might experiment with a few applicants with only one year.

Covid has brought remote work into great attention. The hiring manager must determine how important physical presence is to a particular position. We don't want fire fighters to phone it in, but when a business cannot find people willing to work alone in a cubicle, maybe it's time to allow remote work.

To evaluate remote work rules, the manager needs to estimate the productivity from work performed in the office in relation to the ability to hire people for remote work. Although that is hard to quantify in many cases, rules that limit the pool of job applicants but do not improve productivity will send a company into a downward spiral.

Drug testing is another rule that should be reconsidered. Quest Diagnostics recently reported, "The rate of positive drug test results among America's workforce reached its highest rate last year since

2001." Although nobody wants a stoned employee operating heavy equipment, a positive test for marijuana does not at all imply impairment. A person who tokes pot on Saturday night may be fully alert on Monday morning but still flunk a drug test.

Some companies decided years ago to test all employees. They may have worried about testing some employees, because they operated machinery, but not others who work in the office. Or perhaps they preferred to avoid drug users in all roles. However, the current high incidence of marijuana usage means that such rules will screen out many competent job applicants.

Recruiting is a difficult task in the tight labor market. Business leaders can make their jobs easier by reviewing job requirements and eliminating unnecessary ones.

Resources:

Dick Finnegan wrote: https://c-suiteanalytics.com/job-requirements-vs-the-great-resignation/

The Case Against Education: https://press.princeton.edu/books/hardcover/9780691174655/the-case-against-education

Recent letter to Caplan: https://betonit.substack.com/p/educational-signaling-letter-from-a-disruptor?s=r

Quest Diagnostics recently reported: https://newsroom.questdiagnostics.com/2022-03-30-Workforce-Drug-Test-Positivity-Climbs-to-Highest-Level-in-Two-Decades,-Finds-Quest-Diagnostics-Drug-Testing-Index-Analysis

Chapter 32

What Business Leaders Need To Learn From Harrison Ford And Other Older Workers

Published on Forbes.com July 3, 2023

Harrison Ford at age 80 stars in "Indiana Jones and the Dial of Destiny," just released in theaters. He probably doesn't need the money, his films having grossed over nine billion dollars in total.

More people are working while in their 70s and 80s, according to the Bureau of Labor Statistics. The labor force participation rate—the percentage of people either working or actively looking for a job—for men 75 years of age or older was just 7.1% back in 1987, the earliest data we have. By last year it had risen to 11.2%. That's still a small minority, but a significant change nonetheless. Older women also increased their labor force participation rate, though they are still less likely to work in their older years. All told, we have about one million more employees just from 75+ people being more willing to work.

The issue is important because of the tight labor market. Hiring has become a bit easier in 2023, with more people working or looking for work, but this entire decade is tough. As noted in "The Scariest Chart For Business," the current decade has the lowest growth of the working age population since the Civil War. We have left the era when hiring was easy because of an abundant supply of job applicants. Now hiring and retention have become key skills for business leaders.

Why are older people working? Some need to, given living expenses relative to their Social Security and other income. But some of them work for the satisfaction of getting out of the house and doing something useful. The Wall Street Journal recently profiled several older workers.

A supermarket bakery employee, Andree Carlson, 82, told the Journal that she doesn't need the money. The motivation for her and the other senior citizens is simple: "We like having somewhere to go, something that needs to be done, and everybody likes to feel needed."

Business leaders today should study that simple sentence. "We like having somewhere to go …." People of all ages value the social interaction they have with co-workers and customers. Remote work doesn't get people out of their homes and often does not put them in touch with others. Keep that in mind when thinking about the work environment.

"We like … something that needs to be done …." Younger people call this "purpose." A great opportunity for employers is to identify how the job helps other people. Every job exists for a purpose. The company may be out to make a buck, but that buck is made by satisfying some human need or desire, either directly or indirectly. Whether manufacturing physical products or providing services, someone benefits from the product. Workers in the business-to-business space enable companies that sell directly to consumers. And whether I am buying a meal, an oil change or new underwear, I am better off for having that product—or else I would not have bought it.

"…everybody likes to feel needed." Every manager of every business, non-profit organization and government agency should remember that every morning. Expressing appreciation for the work done by employees will keep the people on the job longer, and with greater engagement.

Older workers can help companies thrive in the tight labor market. And many of them can do a great job. See how Harrison Ford is doing at age 80 in a theater this summer.

Resources:

According to the Bureau of Labor Statistics: https://www.bls.gov/cps/lfcharacteristics.htm#laborforce

The Scariest Chart For Business: https://www.forbes.com/sites/billconerly/2018/03/25/the-scariest-chart-for-business-in-the-coming-decade-workers-not-available/

The Wall Street Journal: https://www.wsj.com/articles/the-reasons-more-people-are-working-in-their-80s-34f11699

Part 6

Conclusion

Conclusion

Business Strategy For The Tight Labor Market

The major themes of these articles are worth restating:

Every employee is an individual. Each person is unique, with a different bundle of strengths, weaknesses, aspirations, worries and personality. Getting great results from any particular employee requires recognition of that person's uniqueness.

First Level Managers are key to employee productivity and retention. That was not my guess when I began studying the subject, but it crops up repeatedly in different ways. As a generalization, it's strong.

Company leadership must motivate first level managers to be great productivity coaches, which includes employee retention. Although it's the first-level managers who are most important, they need support and leadership from senior executives to do their best work. Moreover, they need to be relieved of minor tasks that take time away from productivity coaching.

About the Author

Dr. Bill Conerly connects the dots between the economy and business. He is a business economics consultant, a Senior Contributor to Forbes and a Duke University Ph.D. He has worked in economics and corporate planning at two Fortune 500 corporations and at a major bank, where he was senior vice president.

Companies have used Dr. Conerly's expertise to help with decisions regarding capital expenditures, staffing, inventory levels, expansion into new markets, pricing, business models and financial structure.

Bill Conerly has spoken to over 1400 business audiences in five countries and 31 states, and written two books, including The Flexible Stance: Thriving in a Boom/Bust Economy.

Contact:

Dr. Bill Conerly
503-785-3485
Bill@ConerlyConsulting.com
www.ConerlyConsulting.com

Conerly Consulting LLC
PO Box 2188
Lake Oswego, OR 97035

Made in the USA
Monee, IL
03 November 2026

67387013R00079